I0797729

LEADING YOUR MINISTRY THROUGH ORGANIZATIONAL AND CULTURAL CHANGE

MISSION DESIGN

AARON ABRAMSON

An imprint of InterVarsity Press
Downers Grove, Illinois

InterVarsity Press
P.O. Box 1400 | Downers Grove, IL 60515-1426
ivpress.com | email@ivpress.com

InterVarsity Press® is the publishing division of InterVarsity Christian Fellowship/USA®. For more information, visit intervarsity.org.

While many stories in this book are true, some names and identifying information may have been changed to protect the privacy of individuals.

Cover design: Faceout Studio, Jeff Miller
Interior design: Daniel van Loon
Image: © lvcandy / DigitalVision Vectors via Getty Images

ISBN 978-1-5140-1306-9 (print) | ISBN 978-1-5140-1307-6 (digital)

Printed in Colombia ♾

Library of Congress Cataloging-in-Publication Data
A catalog record for this book is available from the Library of Congress.

31 30 29 28 27 26 25 | 13 12 11 10 9 8 7 6 5 4 3 2 1

This book is dedicated to my wife,

VICTORIA.

Her unwavering support and insightful candor

throughout these years have helped shape me

into the leader I am today.

CONTENTS

INTRODUCTION

"GREAT! So, who is going to take the lead on that?" We had just wrapped up a particularly productive team meeting on how to get local churches in New York involved in reaching out to their Jewish friends and neighbors. We were hammering out the beginnings of a solution when the question came up. Everyone avoided eye contact. None of us had time to add another job to our already overspilling plates.

Ministry can be overwhelming. Over my years serving with Jews for Jesus, I have put in my share of long weeks. I knew when I signed up for ministry that it wasn't going to be easy. It is not unusual for pastors and missionaries (even volunteers) to put in fifty-, sixty-, and even seventy-five-hour workweeks as they try to get their church, their project, their (fill in the blank) off the ground. The work feels never-ending with always one more thing (or ten) to do. Many of us have gotten used to wearing multiple hats as we switch between roles as needed. Project manager, missionary, Bible teacher, scriptwriter, director, web designer, recruiter, fundraiser, painter, worship leader, facilities manager. These are just a few hats I have worn over the years, and I know I'm not the only one.

Ministry staff are typically over-employed, working two, even three jobs. We end up doing whatever is necessary to keep the ministry afloat, despite smaller budgets and strong competition for talent. Let's face it: finding qualified, experienced, capable staff is tough. As writer Kate Shellnutt observed, "For many nonprofits—from sending organizations to food banks—demand is up, and they haven't been able to find enough volunteers to help."[1] The deficit means more work spread among fewer people. Attrition due to burnout, financial constraints, and all sorts of personal reasons only makes things more difficult. According to a 2022 Barna survey done during the height of the Covid pandemic, 42 percent of pastors considered quitting full-time ministry in the twelve months prior to the survey.[2] These findings were not an aberration due to Covid but are consistent with other studies from recent years.

Coupled with the fact that people aren't exactly beating down the door to go into ministry, the need for fresh talent is greater than ever. Many denominations report rapidly declining numbers of incoming clergy.[3] This relates to the concurrent drop in general church attendance. The Church of England has been experiencing this decline for over a decade as over two thousand churches have closed their doors due to shrinking numbers and reduced income.[4]

On top of that, the world is changing at a head-spinning pace. And the rate of change is not showing signs of slowing down. Ray Kurzweil's famous quote, "We won't experience 100 years of progress in the 21st century—it will be more like 20,000 years of progress (at today's rate)" sounds extreme—yet it is hard for most of us to imagine things changing faster than they are now.[5]

To illustrate, macro trends like population growth, technological interconnectedness, and secularization are changing cities from New York to Jerusalem in dramatic ways. Both have sizable ultra-Orthodox Jewish communities, and their birthrate is outpacing other communities around them, causing their neighborhoods to explode at the seams. Yet rabbis in these communities are losing a battle to keep their youth away from smartphones and the internet, and as a result a growing number of Hasidic youth are leaving the Orthodox community to lead secular lives.

Macro trends like these are changing the landscape around us in remarkable ways. This is creating new challenges for us to address as ministers—often before we have been able to solve last month's problems! But if we don't address these challenges promptly and proactively, our current program offerings will eventually become outdated and out of step with our key audiences. Rather than carve out the time to retool, build something new, or even just to *stop* and *reflect* on the situation in which we find ourselves, we end up running back and forth plugging holes like the proverbial Dutch boy trying to stop the dike from breaking.

BEFRIENDING CHANGE

I come naturally to the topic of change. I've always been interested in figuring out how things work. Much to my parents' dismay, I was the kid constantly taking stuff apart at home. I remember disassembling my first PC so I could understand what each component did as well as how each part worked together to make data come to life.

That curiosity was cultivated in a milieu of diverse cultures, beliefs, and cities. As a third culture kid,[6] my world leaned toward change and instability. We never lived in one home for more than a few years. On top of that, I was raised in an intermarried home—my father raised Jewish, and my mother raised Catholic; each brought a mixture of faith and tradition into my life. My friends would ask if I found celebrating both Hanukkah and Christmas confusing. I'd say, "What's confusing about getting presents twice?" The hybridity of an interfaith family was all I knew.

Hungry for a deeper Jewish experience, my parents decided to move us from the United States to Israel. At fifteen years old, I was suddenly and completely immersed in Jewish life. We lived in an Orthodox settlement, and I attended a yeshiva—an Orthodox school for rabbinic studies.

At eighteen, I was drafted into the Israeli army, where my aptitude for tinkering and problem-solving was put to good use. I was trained as a technician on armored transport carriers and served in the 890 paratrooper unit. Unlike the well-equipped US military, we often lacked the right tools for the job, so we learned to improvise on the fly. We did what we had to do to get those transports moving, often under dangerous conditions.

After completing three years of service, I experienced a crisis of purpose and identity, leading me to pack my bags and travel for a year. That year turned into a kind of spiritual wilderness for me. With no job or anything tying me down, there was nothing but time and space to reflect and look inward. The deeper I looked, the more I realized something was wrong. I attempted to apply that problem-solving approach to my own condition. I was reading books ranging from Eastern philosophy to New Age spirituality when a friend suggested I read the New Testament. Immediately I realized there was something different about the Gospels and the Messiah they described. For the next few months, I immersed myself in the Scriptures. The more I read about Jesus, the more I was drawn to him. When God opened my eyes and I surrendered my life to him, I discovered new purpose. He changed me and gave me new lenses through which to view the world.

It became clear early in my faith journey that I longed to share the gospel with other Jewish people. I tried to talk about my new faith with people in Israel, which turned out to be (surprise, surprise!) incredibly difficult. It never occurred to me that there were other people trying to do the same thing I was doing until I met some team members serving with Jews for Jesus. After volunteering for a couple of years, I officially joined the Jews for Jesus staff in 1999 and have served with the organization in a number of different capacities.

I started my training in New York City and served in the UK, where I completed a BA in sociology and theology at All Nations Christian College. I've also worked in San Francisco, Seattle, Tel Aviv, and Jerusalem. I've served as a missionary on the field, director of young adult ministry, director of recruitment, NY regional director, COO, and now CEO—all roles which have required me to lead teams through lots of perplexing situations. Each of these roles came with unique challenges, but all of them had one thing in common: change.

The organization was facing a season of dramatic transition from who we were when Jews for Jesus first started in 1973 to who we needed to become as we moved into the new millennium. Change has been a theme in my life and also the one constant in my vocation. As a result, I've discovered that my long-standing curiosity about the way things work has led me to befriend change—personally, organizationally, and culturally. My trust in the unchanging character of God has been a strength as I've helped lead our organization through significant transition over the last few years.

The rate of change around us doesn't seem to be slowing down anytime soon. If anything, the world is becoming more complex. Peter H. Diamandis and Steven Kotler in their book *The Future is Faster than You Think* explain it this way:

> But now we live in a world that is global and exponential. Global, meaning if it happens on the other side of the planet, we hear about it seconds later (and our computers hear about it only milliseconds later). Exponential, meanwhile, refers to today's blitzkrieg speed of development. Forget about the difference between generations, currently mere months can bring a revolution.[7]

The communities to whom we minister are changing rapidly. How we minister to them requires fresh eyes. Emerging generations of young adults are being raised in a very different world than the one in which I was raised. And now as a father to three kids born in the early 2000s, I can see significant differences in the issues they care about and the way they approach the world. Deep down, at the core, every generation is in need of the same thing: a life-changing encounter with the risen Messiah. But the specific concerns, needs, and desires are constantly changing. That is why the gospel, which doesn't change, is in need of constant contextualization.

When I was a new believer attending church in the late 1990s, homosexuality was rarely discussed. Today it has become one of the most pressing issues in the church. Paul Bond's shocking 2022 *Newsweek* article claimed nearly 30 percent of millennial Christians identified as LGBTQ. A quick survey of Christian attitudes on this topic demonstrates a dramatic shift among younger Christians, with over 50 percent of them in favor of changing laws to support the LGBTQ community compared to 30 percent of those over forty.[8]

David Kinnaman, president of the Barna Group, sums up:

> How the Christian community responds to the LGBTQ community is, in many ways, the defining social and moral issue of the day. Many churches and Christian leaders are going to rise or fall based on how they address it.[9]

If we are going to reach the next generation with the gospel, we need to find a way to present it that speaks to every issue. While we will never compromise the gospel, we also can't simply ignore the need for robust biblical engagement with the world around us. The gospel has answers to the needs of every community, and it's our responsibility to communicate that message in a way that our audience can understand.

While it has never been up to us to "save" anyone, God invites us to partner with him in building his kingdom. He has equipped us with everything we need to fulfill this task (Hebrews 13:20-21). So how do we achieve this? How do we not get sidetracked by the myriad problems we face? How can we remain nimble, faithful, and mission focused as we adapt to a changing world? And how will we know what progress looks like when the results are intangible?

By integrating biblical wisdom, management concepts, and human-centered design principles, this book equips ministry leaders to ask critical questions, hone their vision, generate fresh ideas, and implement solutions to achieve meaningful, lasting kingdom impact. We'll draw relevant examples from both Scripture and the contemporary business, church, and nonprofit world. We will examine change through the principles found in strategic leadership, change management, performance measurement, design thinking, social entrepreneurship, and marketing, all grounded and filtered through the unchanging call of Jesus in every generation to go and make disciples (Matthew 28:18-20).

We will explore how to implement relevant, sustainable change at the heart of your ministry through the creation of an "innovation engine." We will explore how to build this engine through an approach I call Mission Design.

Mission Design is the culmination of what our team learned while grappling with the symptoms of age and decline. It's about how we faced diminished ministry effectiveness and how we began to turn the ship around. In these pages, I've attempted to present an honest and transparent picture of Jews for Jesus, and of my own "always in process" leadership experience. Mission Design is also about how we confronted changing demographics and shifting cultures. How we let go of beloved ministry programs that weren't yielding desired results and rebuilt our mission strategy from the ground up. These aren't all victory stories. Whether you are reviving a well-established mission or launching a brand-new ministry, my hope is that this book can be a helpful resource for you.

HOW THIS BOOK CAN HELP YOU

This isn't a theology book or a missiology book, though there is some theology and missiology in it. This book isn't about the history of missions or even contextualization, though it will touch on these subjects. This isn't exactly a management book either. This book describes how an established organization, Jews for Jesus, had lost momentum and found a way forward in a world of constant flux. It is about the lessons we learned along the way and the tools we developed to help us get there.

But this book isn't about the organization I know. It isn't about the other organizations I reference. If you are an established or emerging leader, a mover and shaker, a thinker, or a dreamer, this book is about you. You are not alone if you are not satisfied with the status quo of the past and want to see change and meaningful growth in your ministry or organization. Whether you are struggling to break away from old patterns or trying to forge new ones, there is a way forward.

In this book, we'll take a closer look at how to cultivate problem-solving techniques and take advantage of the opportunities that exist all around us. We will learn how to get honest feedback so that we can evaluate mission effectiveness and identify challenges head-on. We will look to build on our strengths and shore up our weaknesses. We will take time to learn from our mistakes and seek to hear God's voice throughout the journey. We will learn what it looks like to move forward as an organization.

My hope is that this book can provide helpful tools and fresh perspective to help you design the future of your ministry. May the information and the approaches I've provided, along with the additional tools in the appendixes, help you succeed in the work God has called you to do.

PART 1

THE NEED FOR MISSION DESIGN

ONE

THE LIFE CYCLE OF AN ORGANIZATION

IN 2006, I presented a report to the Jews for Jesus board of directors and senior leadership on the aging demographics of our staff. This report could have been titled, "Where did all the young people go?" The average age of our mission staff was forty-two years old. Simply put, we were struggling to engage the next generation. Recruitment for our programs was in freefall, and the people who were signing up tended to be older adults. For an organization that had built its reputation on street evangelism and campus ministry for over thirty years, these findings were concerning.

There was general agreement among the leadership team that something needed to be done. We met, prayed, discussed, prayed more, and eventually came up with a mission-wide goal to recruit fifty new mission staff in five years. At the time, we were recruiting somewhere between three and five new missionaries each year. Onboarding ten missionaries a year was going to be a tall order. As director of recruitment at the time, I was tasked with leading the charge. I had no idea where to start. I realized very quickly that there was no blueprint or operating manual I could use to solve our recruitment problem.

In the organization's beginning, Jews for Jesus experienced a season of rapid growth fueled by activism, innovation, and youth. Our founder, Moishe Rosen, had been serving with a well-established mission called the American Board of Missions to the

Jews (ABMJ). His desire to see Jewish people come to know Jesus would lead him to venture out of New York City, the hub of American Jewish life, to the California frontier. In the late 1960s and into the early 1970s, the United States was going through a season of immense change. America was being reshaped by cultural shifts stemming from things including, but not limited to, the Vietnam War, the civil rights movement, and the emerging role of women in society.

A passionate, idealistic generation was coming of age, and they saw the world in a radically different way than their parents did. These so-called hippies were leaving home in droves, and California was their destination of choice. Initially Moishe saw them as an irrelevant fringe movement, but he was challenged to rethink his view after speaking at an InterVarsity event at Columbia University. He had told a joke about hippies smelling bad and was challenged by a Jewish social worker named Bob Berk, who asked if Moishe had been close enough to a hippie to smell them. Moishe realized that a significant portion of these hippies were Jewish and quite open to the gospel. He knew his approach to reaching these Jewish people would need to be unorthodox. He wasn't going to be able to reach them with the older, tried-and-true approaches of the ABMJ. This meant his suit and tie had to go, his crew cut and clean-shaven appearance would need to change, and the look and content of tracts and booklets would need to speak the language of youth. Ultimately, this led to his parting ways with the ABMJ and pioneering a new mission organization in the early 1970s called Hineni Ministries.[1]

The phrase "Jews for Jesus" was an early slogan of the organization, but it was so catchy that by 1973 it had become the name. Riding the wave of the Jesus Movement, a counterculture Christian youth revolution that emerged in the United States during the late 1960s and early 1970s,[2] Jews for Jesus, like many other North American ministries, saw a relatively high response rate to the gospel in those days. The startup culture of the new ministry made them extremely agile and adaptable to their cultural surroundings. Jews for Jesus was able to capitalize on the moment with the innovation, activism, and youth that characterized the early days of the movement. Everybody but Moishe was in their early twenties and came ready to change the world. They knew how to talk to their peers. They were already contextualizing the message of the gospel for their audience. Armed with billboards, slogans, and a spirit of activism, they took their new message to the streets where the people they wanted to reach were already gathered. The impact was immediate. Our small team was having thousands of gospel-centered interactions in a year with fellow Jewish hippies, and a multitude of them were coming to the Lord. *Time* magazine even published an article about the growing number of Jewish believers coming to faith in the Messiah during the Jesus Movement.[3]

Fast-forward to 2006. We found ourselves dealing with what many organizations face after the initial launch and growth stages. The momentum of the 1970s had carried us through the '80s and into the '90s, but by the 2010s, we were dealing with the symptoms of decline. We found ourselves trying to deal with the problem of how to recruit young people. We were back at the drawing board asking ourselves, "Where do we go from here?"

In retrospect, I don't believe we were asking the real questions yet. But we were about to discover why we weren't attracting younger people.

LIFE CYCLE STAGES

All organizations have a life cycle, whether they're big or small, new or long-established. Initially in 2006, I hadn't given much thought to where our organization was in its life cycle. I just sensed Jews for Jesus was struggling to find its way forward.

While all organizations are unique, most follow a similar growth trajectory with common phases or stages. Understanding these stages can help leaders gain greater awareness of where their organization is and what it needs to move forward. It can also be helpful in anticipating changes that naturally come with growth. The Georgia Center for Nonprofits offers this list of six common stages in an organization's life cycle:

- ***Idea:*** A small yet committed team identifies a need (or needs) for a specific constituency and envisions a solution to meet that need.
- ***Startup:*** Programs and services are developed and launched to address the needs of its constituents. Starting to develop organizational capacity and experimenting with program design.
- ***Growth:*** As the organization hits its stride, it focuses on standardizing and broadening its programs while formalizing structures and processes to ensure organizational vitality.
- ***Maturity:*** The organization has an established reputation. It is well managed by an executive leader and a board of directors. Structures and processes are aligned with its strategic plan. A mature organization has streamlined its programs and is highly efficient.
- ***Decline:*** The organization has become rigid and slow to change. It is more institutionalized with an increasingly hierarchical leadership structure. It is out of touch with the needs of its constituents and change is slow. The systems and structures act as a barrier hindering growth.
- ***Crisis:*** The organization is experiencing rapid decline. If nothing is done to address it, the organization will hit a point of no return. Leadership is struggling, attrition is high, and funding is waning. The organization has several options: close down, merge with another organization, or do the difficult work of a complete overhaul.[4]

The energy and vision of the early days of an organization can't last forever. We all age. Fatigue sets in, staff leave, new staff join, programs get stale, and the world keeps moving forward. Over time, even small, incremental shifts create misalignment. Without intervention, it's easy to slip into this rut—and all organizations and ministries are

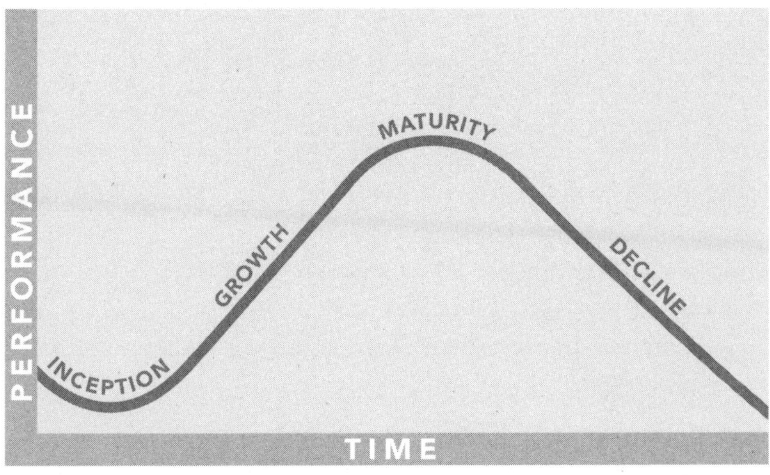

Figure 1.1. Business performance over time[5]

vulnerable to this struggle. The church up the street from where we lived in Manhattan once packed over a thousand into its sanctuary each week, but today they rent out the building on Sunday to keep the doors open for a handful of remaining members.

Various denominational studies have been done on this trend. The Redeemer City to City church planting network compared the effectiveness of new church plants over long-term churches: "The average new congregation will bring six to eight times more new people into the life of the body of Christ than an older congregation of the same size."[6] One key reason points to the life cycle of an organization. Young ministries tend to be adaptable, agile, and experimental in nature. That innovative spirit leads to greater ministry effectiveness.

Jews for Jesus was no exception. The innovation that characterized our early years was wearing off, and we were slipping into a pattern of slow decline. But was it inevitable? Must all organizations cycle into decline? Both startups and well-established organizations can experience stagnation, but it often takes years to get to the Crisis Stage. Susan Kenny Stevens, founder of the Nonprofit Lifecycles Institute, describes a turnaround point where organizations can avoid the Crisis Stage through strong leadership and a committed board of

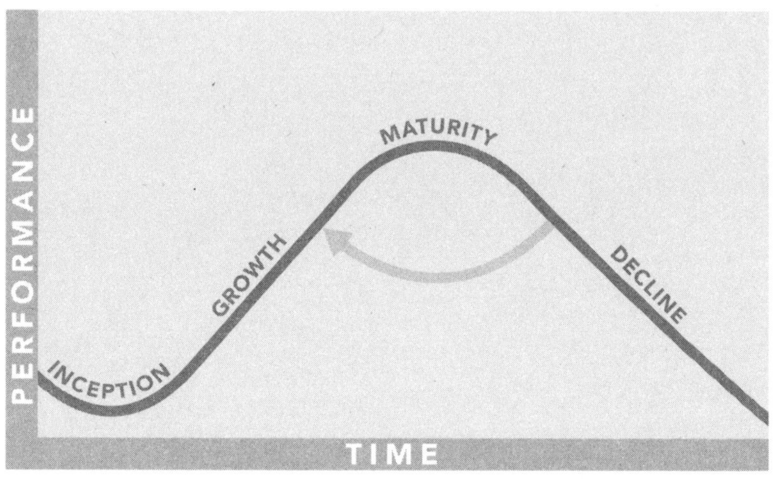

Figure 1.2. Turnaround point for businesses in decline[7]

directors willing to do what it takes to reposition the organization for growth.[8]

This process is painful, and it requires strong leadership willing to make tough, uncomfortable decisions. These decisions will likely involve a combination of financial cuts, staff cuts, and programming changes.

This kind of chart is often referred to as a sigmoid curve or bell curve. For an organization to thrive and avoid long-term decline, it needs to launch another sigmoid curve. This means bringing new vitality back into the organization. This is far easier to do when momentum is on the upswing.[9]

Initially, change may lead to a decline in performance, as it takes time to adapt and build momentum again. But the result is a revitalized organization with a new growth plan.

A startup organization is like a new movement. Team members are highly committed and invested in the cause. They are willing to commit personal time and resources for the greater good. The structure tends to be fluid, and leadership is typically shared. But over time, even the most dynamic movements naturally begin to shift toward becoming institutions. This is because every organization

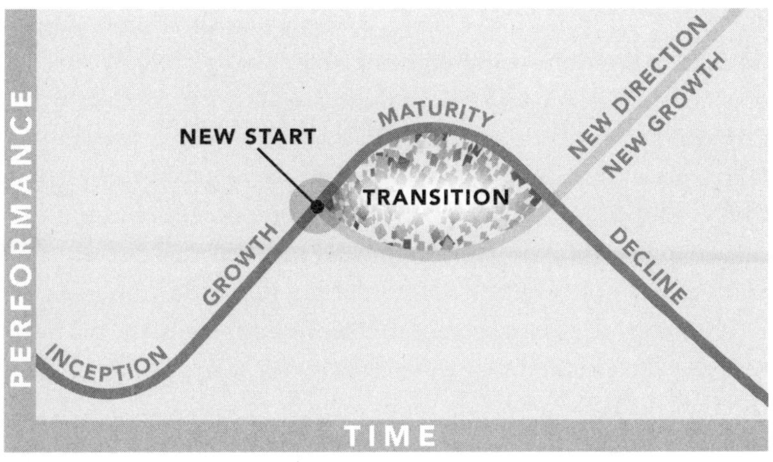

Figure 1.3. Relaunching a sigmoid curve[10]

needs stability and structure in order to survive. Without things like 401(k)s, HR departments, and long-term plans, movements lack consistency and eventually peter out.

That is why the ideal organization falls somewhere between a movement and an institution. Turning an organization around is about bringing the movement back into an institution.[11] Tim Keller put it like this: "A strong movement, then, occupies the difficult space between being a free-wheeling organism and a disciplined organization. A movement that refuses to take on some organizational characteristics—authority, tradition, unity of belief, and quality control—will fragment and dissipate."[12]

We all long to experience movement in our ministries. Being part of a movement is exciting and life-giving. It brings enthusiastic, motivated people together around a common vision. But once that energy is gone, building it back into your organization takes a lot of work. If that is where your ministry is at, don't despair. It is possible to inject movement back into your mission! I saw it happen in Jews for Jesus. That isn't to say it was easy. It wasn't. But change is possible.

An essential part of navigating change is understanding the moment we're in and discerning the need for change both within our organization and in the world. If we hope to turn things around, we need to develop an awareness of what is happening. We need a grasp of the cultural and spiritual climate in which we serve so we can better assess the context in which our organization's change is taking place. This means listening and interacting with those in our own organizations and those we seek to reach. The insights and reflections we glean should be tempered with spiritual discernment and a broader view of God's movement in the world around us.

If we hope to see movement in the right direction, we will need to count the cost and take the necessary steps to see this process through. And it is important for us to begin to understand how our staff, no matter how successful they have been in the past, may react to change.

Even desired change.

DISCUSSION QUESTIONS

- Where is your church or organization in its life cycle? Where would you prefer to be? Why?
- Is there agreement among your leadership about where your organization is at in its life cycle?
- What has changed in your ministry context that necessitates a new approach to ministry?

TWO

REACTIONS TO CHANGE

OUR BOARD OF DIRECTORS and senior leadership were in agreement. The lack of younger staff was an urgent problem that needed to be addressed immediately. It was 2006 and we were struggling to recruit Millennials. We all recognized that the future of our organization was at stake. I knew that if we were going to make sense of the problem, we would need to start by talking to lots of people from this age demographic. So I spent hours interviewing Jewish believers in Jesus between the ages of eighteen and twenty-six, meeting in person whenever possible. I wanted to understand how they experienced Jews for Jesus. I read many studies on Millennials and Jewish Millennials. I was doing everything I could to get more clarity on what was happening.

The feedback I received was sobering. Most of the people I interviewed had negative impressions of Jews for Jesus that had been shaped by things they had heard in the past. Very few had personal experience. The issue seemed to be reputation. The majority felt we were simply irrelevant. We were out of step with the current culture and had little to offer them. It was clear that if Jews for Jesus was going to be a place for them to serve, we would need to make some drastic changes.

Up until this point, Jews for Jesus had mainly been known for high-visibility evangelistic campaigns. Between twenty and thirty Jewish followers of Jesus would blanket the streets in bright Jews for Jesus T-shirts while handing out millions of colorful tracts (called broadsides) in cities with large Jewish populations around the world. Our mission statement was "to make the Messiahship of Jesus an unavoidable issue to our Jewish people worldwide" and we worked hard to get noticed. New York was where we hosted our largest outreach event of the year. We advertised on massive billboards throughout the city with head-turning hooks like *Be more Jewish, believe in Jesus*, and *Jesus made me kosher*. We would pay for full-page ads in the *New York Times* and the *Wall Street Journal*. We had been an annual fixture on the streets and subway stations of New York City every July since 1974. Our goal each summer was the same: hand out as many tracts as possible and talk to as many Jewish people as possible about Jesus. Through these campaigns, our teams would interact with thousands of Jewish people, and we were able to follow up with many throughout the year.

While our literature and approach were designed to reach Jewish people, we shared the gospel with everyone. We were so ubiquitous that it was not uncommon for us to make headlines in newspapers or Jewish publications. The police knew we were coming, the Port Authority knew we were coming, and most importantly, the Jewish community knew we were coming. Our approach in those days was a well-oiled machine geared to introduce Jesus to as many Jewish people as we were able. For better or worse, this style of outreach wasn't just *associated with* our brand; it *was* our brand. We had become synonymous with this style of evangelistic outreach. That was what we were known for, and the next generation was struggling to relate to it.

As I tried to make sense of the problems we were facing, I discovered I wasn't alone. Many Jewish and Christian organizations were wrestling with similar questions. Everyone seemed to be asking how we could understand and engage the next generation. It was apparent that the world was shifting. Everyone was feeling the accelerated pace of cultural and technological change. John Kotter, professor emeritus at Harvard Business School and author of *Leading Change* wrote in 2012, "Today any company that isn't rethinking its direction at least every few years—as well as constantly adjusting to changing contexts—and then quickly making significant operational changes is putting itself at risk."[1] For many organizations, the five-year plan has become the two-year plan as the task of forecasting five or ten years out seems unrealistic if not impossible.

Months of research led me to the beginning of a solution to our problem. I proposed we prioritize investing in the next generation through a blend of discipleship, Jewish identity formation, and practical ministry exposure. Instead of expecting them to fit into our long-standing programs, we would launch a discipleship program oriented to the needs of young Jewish Millennials. I called the initiative Massah (the Hebrew word for a journey). I pitched my proposal for Massah to the leadership of Jews for Jesus. I don't remember the specific responses I received that day, but my overall recollection of those meetings was that I left feeling deflated.

It wasn't that I was being told I couldn't prototype my ideas or that leadership was in disagreement with me. In fact, I had the complete support of our executive director, David Brickner. I was disappointed in the muted enthusiasm my proposal had received. Instead of excitement, it felt like staff had questions and concerns. They wanted to know things like, "How much is it going to cost?" and "Is this going to divide our recruitment focus to the detriment of other programs?" and most importantly "Is this going to replace evangelistic campaigns?" These weren't unfair questions. In fact, these were pretty normal questions. I just didn't have enough experience at the time to anticipate that type of reaction.

In retrospect, I should have expected questions and even criticism when proposing something different. It's not unusual when sharing new ideas; even good ideas receive pushback. J. K. Rowling's manuscript for *Harry Potter and the Philosopher's Stone* had been rejected twelve times before a publisher finally accepted it. Imagine how she felt by the thirteenth publisher! Innovation requires tenacity, grit, and a thick skin.

Despite the lukewarm reaction my initial proposal received, I got the green light to launch our first Massah program the next summer. Thirteen Jewish believing young adults spent the summer in Israel growing in their faith, exploring Jewish identity, and getting ministry experience. While it wasn't a perfect summer, we received overwhelmingly positive feedback, and the word spread. We began to compile a growing list of young adults who were excited about participating in Massah the following year.

At our next leadership gathering, I was excited to share the results of the first Massah prototype. Once again, I felt disappointed by the response. I was hoping for some acknowledgment for launching a successful new program, which in hindsight was not a realistic expectation. Instead, I once again received a slew of uneasy questions like, "Why haven't you recruited as many young adults for the New York Summer Campaign?" and "Have you spent enough time recruiting for our other programs?"

I thought I was putting together a new ministry program to help solve our recruiting problem, but what I was actually doing without realizing it at the time was introducing change to an organization that was used to doing things a certain way. Change, even the most necessary change, challenges everyone in an organization.

One of my favorite examples of this in Scripture is found in the story of God's redemption of Israel from 430 years of slavery in Egypt. The Hebrew people were desperate for things to change: "The people of Israel groaned because of their slavery and cried out for help. Their cry for rescue from slavery came up to God" (Exodus 2:23). They were begging for change. The Lord told Moses he had heard the cries of his people and was concerned for their suffering (Exodus 3:7). But when God miraculously delivered his chosen people from bondage, their response to their dramatic change in status showed their disorientation and resistance to the change for which they'd longed:

> When Pharaoh drew near, the people of Israel lifted up their eyes, and behold, the Egyptians were marching after them, and they feared greatly. And the people of Israel cried out to the Lord. They said to Moses, "Is it because there are no graves in Egypt that you have taken us away to die in the wilderness? What have you done to us in bringing us out of Egypt? Is not this what we said to you in Egypt: 'Leave us alone that we may serve the Egyptians'? For it would have been better for us to serve the Egyptians than to die in the wilderness." (Exodus 14:10-12)

Their deliverance wasn't a tidy new beginning. Their past was literally chasing them. Pharaoh and his army were pursuing them into the wilderness. The reaction of the Hebrew people to both their change of status and the challenge of being pursued by their captors is as familiar as the reactions of leaders when change comes to their organizations today. Let's take a moment to look at these reactions.

- ***Panic:*** Change leads us into the unknown, and we can expect to encounter new problems. When a threat looms, fear is a normal response. It is natural for people to panic when things go wrong. A wise leader anticipates it. Levelheaded leadership can make a huge difference when panic begins to set in.
- ***Second-guessing:*** Yesterday, getting out of Egypt was the best idea ever. But a day out of Egypt and the Israelites are ready to throw in the towel. Leaving went from the best idea to the worst idea. When problems arise, it is common to hear things like, "I told you this was going to happen," or "I knew it wouldn't work."
- ***Doubt:*** With the first sign of trouble, the people blamed Moses. When problems arise, people are quick to doubt and find fault with the leadership that has led them into the unknown.

- ***A desire to go back to the way things were:*** Within hours, the people of Israel regretted leaving Egypt: "It would have been better for us to serve the Egyptians" (Exodus 14:12). People are often more willing to cope with familiar problems (even big ones) than the possibility of new, unknown ones.

Change is first perceived as loss. It was for the Hebrew people as they left Egypt, and it is for those we serve in our organizations. If we are to lead our teams into the unknown, we must count the cost of such a difficult undertaking—and that cost includes the loss of comfort that comes with the familiar.

My experience with introducing Massah taught me to recognize that some of the resistance I faced was an expression of loss. And I needed to learn some hard lessons about the emotional landscape of change and loss so I wouldn't take resistance personally. Change is coming for us all, and learning how to lead with compassion and wisdom can keep an organization moving forward even when many may be asking to return to an Egypt that is no longer home.

WISDOM FOR NAVIGATING CHANGE

The statistics on organizational change are sobering. John Kotter's 1996 research *Leading Change* revealed that roughly 30 percent of change programs succeed.[2] In a similar study from 2008, McKinsey surveyed 3,199 executives around the world and found, as Kotter did, that only one in three change transitions succeeds.[3] These figures aren't meant to deter or discourage you. They are meant to paint a realistic picture of the challenges of managing change. That is why it is essential that we seek God's direction in our lives and in our ministries. We must never underestimate the power of prayer, God's Word, and the wisdom of the people he has put in our lives. He wants us to ask him. He isn't withholding wisdom from us. James 1:5 tells us, "If any of you lacks wisdom, let him ask God, who gives generously to all without reproach, and it will be given him." He is faithful to guide us toward wisdom, both individually and corporately.

Back when I was grappling with our recruitment problem and couldn't make sense of what to do next, a local pastor asked me what was keeping me up at night. I told him about our challenges engaging young adults, feeling stuck, and having no idea how to solve the problem. After listening for a while he said, "Aaron, you're pregnant." He had my attention. He then shared words from Isaiah 66:9: "Do I bring to the moment of birth and not give delivery?" (NIV). This reference to God's redemptive plan for Israel and his faithfulness to bring his plans to fruition helped me put my own struggles into perspective. When I feel uncertain or anxious about the future, I am reminded of his Word. It is the Lord that directs our steps.

Wisdom is like a lighthouse that guides us through dark and dangerous waters toward a new destination. We have already received powerful sources of wisdom through God's Son, the Holy Spirit, and his living Word, the Bible. I am continually amazed that God teaches, guides, counsels, and convicts us in wisdom through all sorts of sources, if we remain open to seeking him first and foremost. I can't count the times I have been impacted by a conversation, an article, a piece of art, a song, a view. Solomon even looked to the bugs on the ground for wisdom.

Those of us leading change need all the wisdom we can get, even if that means utilizing tools from outside our faith-based comfort zones—specifically tools designed and used by the business world. We can glean practical wisdom from some of them and utilize them for kingdom purposes.

After leading Israel out of Egypt and through the Red Sea, Moses met up with his father-in-law Jethro and shared everything that had happened, sparing no detail. Pharaoh, the plagues, the parting of the sea, hardships endured. Jethro, amazed, couldn't help but recognize the hand of God in all of this. The following day, after watching Moses deal with problems "from morning till evening," Jethro told Moses, "'What you are doing is not good. You and the people with you will certainly wear yourselves out, for the thing is too heavy for you. You are not able to do it alone" (Exodus 18:13, 17-18). Jethro gave Moses some good leadership coaching. Moses heeded the advice and made his job a bit more manageable.

Moses wasn't aware of how unsustainable his situation was. He was busy doing his job. Only after hearing an alternate perspective from his father-in-law, a chief and leader of a different people, was he able to see what he was doing wrong. Navigating change is complex, and if we are going to succeed, we need to take all the help we can get. Even if it means taking advice from a priest of Midian.

We should always be grounded in Scripture, guided by prayer, and reminded of God's work in our lives. But we should also be open to learning from best practices in business and culture.

There are plenty of good resources that can help us through the change process. Kotter's steps for managing change and William Bridge's transition model are just two useful tools to help organizations navigate change.

Change is difficult even when it's going well. Don't be discouraged if the process takes longer than you initially anticipate. There will be temptation to "return to Egypt" as problems emerge, but if you can stay the course and continue to seek wisdom each step of the journey, change is possible. But before you can begin the change process, it's important to assess the health and effectiveness of your current organization.

DISCUSSION QUESTIONS

- How do you personally respond to change? Do you tend to perceive it as loss? How do you think your response to change has an impact on your church/organization?

- Taking a look at the reactions of the Israelites in Exodus 14, have you experienced similar reactions when trying to start something new? How did you respond?

Take time to pray alone or with your team for wisdom and discernment in navigating change (Deuteronomy 31:6; Ecclesiastes 3:1; Isaiah 43:19; Proverbs 19:21).

THREE

GETTING UNSTUCK

AFTER SIX FRUITFUL YEARS in San Francisco, Victoria and I were moving back to New York City with our three young children. Jews for Jesus had been looking for a new leader for its New York chapter, and I had been offered the job. We'd lived and ministered in New York from 2000 to 2003, during and after 9/11. We were exhausted by the time we left and never imagined returning. But we accepted the call and packed our bags.

When we returned in 2009, I was surprised at how much things had changed since we left. It was the same bustling metropolis, full of people from all over the world trying to make it to the top. Doctors, artists, brokers, designers, lawyers, entrepreneurs, chefs, you name it—they ended up in New York. But the world had changed. We had fully entered the digital age, and people were interacting in new ways. Street evangelism, once a mainstay of the ministry of Jews for Jesus, had become far more difficult. People were plugged in, logged on, scrolling through social feeds, texting, chatting with friends, listening to podcasts and audiobooks, streaming music, and watching videos on demand. The busy, distracted city had become busier and more distracted.

It also became apparent that Jewish people were avoiding us. Our style of evangelism wasn't producing the same results as in previous decades. New York was home to over two million Jewish people—the largest Jewish population outside of Israel—but we were struggling to find people to whom we could minister. Our mission had become less relevant and less engaged with the people I had moved across the country to reach.

DIAGNOSING THE PROBLEM

It's one thing to know there is a problem, but it's entirely another to know what to do about it. I was a trained missionary. Like many of my colleagues, I had studied subjects like theology, hermeneutics, Greek, Hebrew, homiletics, and missiology. My training hadn't prepared me to diagnose and solve the kinds of problems we were facing in New York City.

Amer Olson, a longtime friend and colleague, had relocated to New York at the same time we did. He is a talented artist, a Jewish believer in Jesus, and also had a young and growing family at the time. Together we were trying to make sense of the city and to figure out what we needed to do to get the team on track. The good news was that we were a team of dedicated ministers; the bad news was that we were a team of dedicated ministers. As missionaries, we were called and ready to do whatever was necessary to make a kingdom impact. The problem was that we lacked experience and expertise to navigate organizational change.

Don't misunderstand me. God's calling and empowerment will always be the single most important qualification for ministry. There is no substitute for the passion and purpose of those he has called. He continues to use men and women to build his kingdom regardless of training or skills. But that doesn't change the fact that many ministers, pastors, and missionaries are typically seminary grads. They are rarely trained to run the business side of an organization yet are often required to do so.

To complicate matters further, the vast majority of ministries have tiny budgets and very few staff. To put this into perspective, the average church in the United States has sixty-five congregants and an annual income of $120,000.[1] Many of these churches have one paid minister running a gamut of programs, preaching sermons, meeting people, performing weddings, overseeing a facility, and a thousand other tasks. Most ministries lack the staff and resources to begin redesigning programs or launching new ones. Ministers are usually so busy they don't have time to stop, ponder, identify, and solve the most important questions their ministry is facing.

Our small staff in New York was no different. I began with and continued in prayer. Walking city streets has long been my favorite way to pray. I have prayed for wisdom while wandering the streets of many cities around the world. This time, I was wandering through New York, praying. As the weeks went by, I watched in gratitude as God sent me two helpful resources in response to my cries for his help.

The first was the Redeemer City to City church planting network (redeemercitytocity.com). Though they now offer programs for parachurch organizations, at the time City to City only worked with congregations, so Amer and I weren't able to participate in a church planting cohort, but we benefited from bimonthly City Lab events. The late pastor Tim Keller would present topics from his book *Center Church: Doing Balanced, Gospel-Centered Ministry in Your City* to New York–based ministry leaders, and we would break into groups for discussion. *Center Church* is a useful book written to help ministers better contextualize the gospel and reach people in their city.

Processing big questions with other New York–based ministers was a wonderful experience. The goal was to help leaders develop a "theological vision" for their ministry. Tim Keller and City to City describe it in the following way: "Theological Vision is a faithful restatement of the gospel that reflects a particular type of culture at a specific moment in history. This faithful restatement of the gospel has deep implications for life, ministry and mission."[2] The idea is to gain a deeper understanding of the gospel and its implications for the city where you serve while discerning where God is at work in the church at large. These events coupled with the *Center Church* approach were extremely helpful to us as we grappled with what God was doing among the Jewish people in New York City.

The second resource came to me in the form of a masters of public administration program at New York University. In the course of my studies, I met leaders throughout the nonprofit sector. I also met lots of Jewish people, which was why I had come to New York in the first place. It was an amazing opportunity to discuss leadership challenges with people from different perspectives. Everyone was passionate about changing the world, and while most didn't agree with my views, they related to me as a peer and engaged with my ideas. The assigned readings were practical and class interaction was stimulating. The program covered a range of subjects, including strategic leadership, change management, nonprofit finance, budgeting, communications, marketing, board governance, and performance measurement. While there, I encountered two management tools that I have found especially useful in navigating complex ministry challenges that require organizational transformation: adaptive leadership and design thinking.

ADAPTIVE LEADERSHIP

First posited in the 1990s by Dr. Ron Heifetz, adaptive leadership distinguishes between *technical problems* and *adaptive challenges*. Technical problems are typically easy to identify and can be solved through a combination of time, money, and expertise. They have concrete, clear solutions. A flat tire or a dead laptop are examples of technical problems. There is someone you can call who can fix it. When you solve a technical problem, things go back to the way they were.

Adaptive challenges are complex, multifaceted problems with no obvious answers. They can be difficult to define. They may force us to reconsider our values and see things from different perspectives. Adaptive challenges typically require a mindset shift. Examples might include a gradual drop in church attendance or a manager mediating a staff conflict.

Heifetz argues, "The most common cause of failure in leadership is produced by treating adaptive challenges as if they were technical problems."[3] The solution is not as simple as better church advertising or telling staff workers to follow policy or work out their problems. These kinds of challenges demand emotional intelligence. They require extra care and deliberation.

It is important to understand that most problems are a mix of some technical and some adaptive elements. If you see a doctor and they tell you that your blood pressure is high, they may tell you to take blood pressure medication (technical) and recommend lifestyle changes such as working less or exercising regularly (adaptive). Understanding the difference has been invaluable as I've approached complex ministry challenges.

DESIGN THINKING

I signed up for the course called Design Thinking without knowing exactly what the subject was. It sounded intriguing. The class was led by a team from Ideo, a design consultancy that developed Design Thinking to help businesses, nonprofits, and governments solve problems.

Design Thinking is a problem-solving approach that puts people and their needs front and center. Rather than starting with a thing—such as a Bible study, a video, or a building—it begins by empathizing with and understanding the people you are trying to serve. The idea is to look for patterns, responses, and insights into who they are and what their needs are. This kind of exploration can lead to new opportunities and breakthrough solutions to address those needs.

Design Thinking would ultimately prove to be immensely useful to my team—and eventually the broader ministry of Jews for Jesus—as we sought ways to innovate and redesign aspects of our mission.

Of course, there is no shortage of content out there discussing business innovation, change management, and leadership. Stop in any bookstore and you will see a slew of new titles and magazines featuring the stories of successful CEOs who have "figured it out." There are lots of tools out there in the for-profit world, as intense competition for market share necessitates that businesses and leaders constantly adapt.

But in my experience, the ministry world is often playing catch-up, several steps behind when it comes to grappling with new approaches to navigating change and innovation. In the next section of the book, I have synthesized several models I have found most helpful into the approach I call Mission Design. Mission Design is a toolbox of useful leadership strategies that will help you ask better questions as you seek to make sense of your ministry. It will then help you design, prototype, evaluate, and implement solutions to better achieve the mission God has called you to.

In the following section, I will unpack the Mission Design approach in more depth. Here is a quick look at the Mission Design framework.

Launch: Identify and define. This stage is all about understanding where you are headed. In order to launch (or relaunch) your mission, you must start with a *vision*, a *people*, and an *identity*.

Explore: Empathize and understand. To best serve your community, you need an understanding of who they are and what they care about. That means spending time with them, talking with them, reading what they read, listening to what they listen to, and understanding their values. Only after you understand who they are and what they need can you begin to design solutions to meet those needs.

Reentry: Design and develop. In the Design Stage, we bring our findings back down to earth. We take what we have learned about our key audiences and begin to generate ideas and solutions. Each member has the potential to make a significant contribution. We will look at how to brainstorm and test ideas, and equally important, how to evaluate and identify the winners and the losers. After all, no one wants to waste time on unproductive programs.

Land the ship: Refine and implement. In this stage, everything comes together. Once we have a number of tested ideas, we can begin to prototype, refine, and roll them out. These ideas become part of the core program. The process is iterative as we continue to learn and make adjustments where needed.

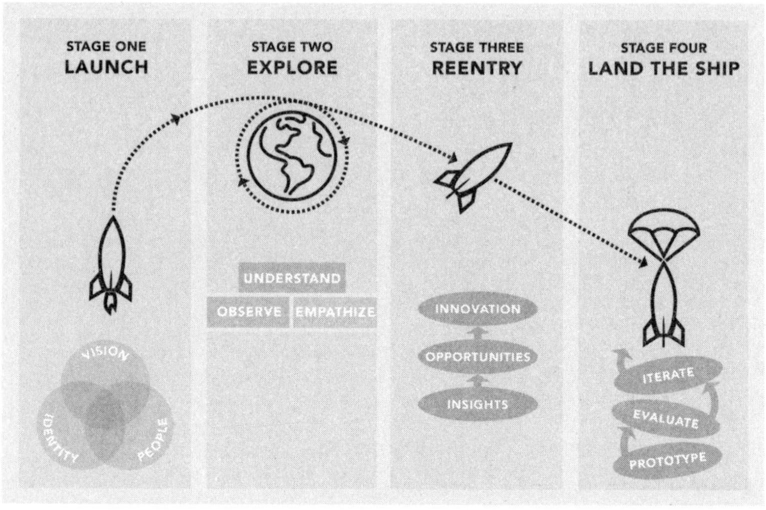

Figure 3.1. Mission Design framework

There are many examples of well-established companies that have used these design principles to develop their business model, including Netflix, Amazon, and Uber. Back in 2009, Airbnb was only making around $200 per week in revenue (that is not a typo). People had a hard time trusting that it would be safe to stay in someone else's property or to share a room in their house. Joe Gebbia, one of the cofounders of Airbnb, noticed that people were posting dark and blurry images of their property listings and realized that may have been contributing to the problem. He then traveled to New York, where he took high-quality images of the rentals. After posting the new images, their weekly revenue doubled.[4]

Mission Design utilizes the same design principles that helped each of these companies refine their core business, understand their customers, prototype potential solutions, test the results, and implement their strategy.

Each stage of Mission Design builds on the others. While it isn't ideal to skip stages, I encourage you to explore the other stages as you go. This process is meant to be dynamic and alive. It doesn't work when things become overly rigid and linear. With these things in mind, let's take a closer look at the first stage of Mission Design, Mission Launch.

DISCUSSION QUESTIONS

- In your current role, list out some of the major problems you or your team have faced. Would you describe them as technical problems or adaptive challenges?
- Have you attempted to solve an adaptive challenge with a technical solution? What happened?

PART 2

THE STAGES OF MISSION DESIGN

FOUR

LAUNCH STAGE PART 1

MISSION—WHAT IS OUR PURPOSE?

A good mission has a finish line—you must be able to know when you've done it, like the moon mission or a mountaintop.

Jim Collins

IF YOU HAVE EVER WATCHED NASA or SpaceX launch a rocket into space, you probably remember a familiar picture. People running around, command teams monitoring systems in a large room, engineers checking numbers and recalculating, everyone looking extremely focused. What you don't see are the years of planning that set all that into motion. It started with someone, or a group of people, who had a dream of going to the moon or of launching a telescope that could look deeper into space than ever before. This idea is immortalized in Neil Armstrong's words, "One small step for a man, one giant leap for mankind." The mission was never just to go to the moon. They believed they were changing lives for the better on earth. They had a mission that drove them forward.

Mission is a murky term that is often discussed when an organization is crafting their mission statement. But figuring out how to communicate why you exist to others isn't the time to begin thinking about your mission. You and your team need to be thinking about where you are headed and the "why" behind your idea right from the beginning. You want to clarify what you hope to accomplish and why it matters. But before you pour time, energy, and money into a new program or into redesigning your current ministry, you need to think through who you are and what you're called to do.

In 2016, Jews for Jesus was nearing the end of its multiyear evangelistic campaign called Behold Your God (BYG). The goal of BYG was to share the gospel with Jewish people in every major Jewish population center around the world. Our strategy had been straightforward: launch large-scale evangelistic campaigns in each of these key cities. We had completed sixty-five campaigns, and our final city was Jerusalem. I had lived in Jerusalem for many years and was well aware of how difficult it was going to be for Jews for Jesus to make any headway there—the largest city in Israel with a Jewish population of nearly six hundred thousand and the largest Orthodox community in the world. It felt like we were standing in front of Mount Everest without a clear way forward.

One thing we knew was that if we took our usual approach of street ministry and tract distribution, the campaign would likely last one day, two at most. We had lots of experience leading outreaches in cities like Paris, London, Boston, and Tel Aviv. Jerusalem was a completely different kind of challenge. The religious presence there was far stronger than in any other city we had been to. Orthodox Jewish people are largely hostile to mission efforts. There are a number of Orthodox organizations that actively search for the slightest hint of missionary activity so they can expose, stop, or even attack them.

We knew we would need another approach if we hoped to find and minister to the people we were hoping to reach.

I arrived in Jerusalem with two experienced leaders, Karol Joseph and Yoel Ben David. They had asked me to help lead this project a couple of months before. Initially I was reluctant to join them as I had my hands full with ministry responsibilities in New

York. To be honest, I didn't really want to be involved. I still had flashbacks of missionaries being physically attacked and chased out of the city of Jerusalem. I remember watching two missionaries jump into a taxi which was then surrounded by an angry mob who attempted to overturn the vehicle to get them out.

We knew we were not there for everyone. We were there to reach those God was drawing to himself. From experience, we knew there are always Jewish people searching and open to the gospel. We just had to find them.

Though we all knew Jerusalem well, we began by spending time getting a feel for the city. We walked the streets, sat in cafés, talked with people, and observed the way people interacted with one another. We spent time praying and reading the Scriptures while staying sensitive to how God was already at work in this incredible place. As we watched, insights began to emerge. We noticed children wandering around freely. We noticed how observant and nonobservant Jews interacted with one another. We saw how Orthodox men and women lived very different lives. We discovered a tight-knit secular subculture that had very different values than its far more religious neighbors.

As we began to get a sense of the city, we realized we were still struggling to clarify our mission. We had been asked to lead a month-long outreach in Jerusalem, but what we were really attempting to accomplish was still fuzzy. Were we really hoping to share the gospel with everyone? Was that even realistic?

So who exactly were we trying to reach? Orthodox Jewish people, secular Jewish people, immigrants, students, families? Did we hope to share the gospel? To disciple them? All our previous BYG campaigns had attempted to reach as many of the Jewish people as possible in those cities, but we hadn't developed a long-term vision for the vast majority of those Jewish communities.

We were beginning to develop a long-term vision for Jerusalem. We were discussing the outcomes we hoped to accomplish and the people we hoped to reach. We knew if we wanted to make noise and get noticed, that wouldn't be difficult. But we all sensed that God was doing something bigger. God was giving us a glimpse of something more lasting.

We began to map out the city and its various communities, and we realized we would need to narrow our focus. There was simply no way to wrap our minds around the needs of six hundred thousand people.

The sheer size of the challenge forced us to ask what we were trying to accomplish. We had been looking for clarity around the destination. Before we could set a path forward and begin our steep climb up Everest, we first needed to figure out what our Everest was. We needed to clarify our mission.

Knowing why you exist and the difference you will make is at the heart of your mission.

DEFINING MISSION

Today *mission* is a popular business term. Most established organizations have mission statements and define their purpose or reason for existence in terms of mission. But the word originated from the Latin *missio* and described the religious practice of the Jesuit order that sent monks out to other people to spread the gospel.[1]

Peter Drucker, largely recognized as the father of modern management, adapted the term for business leaders. Working as a management consultant in 1974, he began advising business leaders to define their "mission—the organization's purpose and very reason for being."[2] Drucker popularized the concept of a corporate mission statement, which became common for businesses to craft in the 1980s.

But there are many ways to talk about mission. Jim Collins and Jerry Porras refer to mission as your organization's "core purpose." Unlike a goal or a strategic initiative, your mission or reason for existence isn't something you expect to fulfill. They write, "Purpose (which should last 100 years) should not be confused with specific goals or business strategies (which should change many times in 100 years). Whereas you might achieve a goal or complete a strategy, you cannot fulfill a purpose; it is like a guiding star on the horizon—forever pursued but never reached."[3]

Believers in Jesus have been assigned a mission. We are guided by the words of Jesus found in Matthew 28:18-20. The great co-mission has been driving the church for two thousand years to go and make disciples. But that command is incredibly broad. If a Christian shelter for battered women or a Bible college both simply defined their mission as "making disciples" without any other description, no one would understand the difference between those incredibly unique ministries.

Before launching anything, it's important to clarify your mission. Called to what? Called to whom? You need to understand why you exist. What difference do you hope to make in the world, and how do you intend to do it? To help think about this, consider these three necessary ingredients:

1 Vision **2** Identity **3** People

Using the analogy of the rocket, think of **vision** as the destination, the place you want to end up. The impact you hope to achieve. Think of your **identity** as who you are: your crew, the people with different roles to play to make it happen. And finally think of the **people** you are launching this mission for in the first place: the ones you are there to serve.

Mission can be found at the nexus of these parts. Together they give us direction and point us to our Everest. But it starts with vision.

DISCUSSION QUESTIONS

- What is the current mission statement of your church or organization?
- In what ways does your programming match your mission statement?
- Do you have programs that don't seem to match that mission? If so, do you think the mission statement should be changed to incorporate those programs or vice versa?

FIVE

LAUNCH STAGE PART 2

VISION—WHERE ARE WE GOING?

WHEN WE THINK OF THE iPOD, the name Steve Jobs comes to mind. But it was Tony Fadell, a diagnostics engineer, who was actually behind the creation of the iPod. Tony had worked for various Silicon Valley companies before joining Apple. He had spent years building numerous handheld devices for companies like Philips, General Magic, Sony, and Toshiba. While working for Philips, he got the idea for a handheld audio player while working on a project with then young startup Audible.

At the end of the twentieth century, people used to buy music in the form of compact discs (CDs). If you wanted to take music with you on the go, you would need to put your CDs in binders, which were large and cumbersome. Audiobooks often required many CDs. If you wanted to take one book on the road, you could be taking ten or twelve CDs with you. Tony wondered how to eliminate the need to carry around CDs. He thought, *What if we created a pocket-size device that could hold the data from hundreds of audiobooks and songs?* He spent years pitching and failing before he brought his project to Apple, where it eventually became a reality. Steve Jobs saw the potential of Tony's vision, which was eventually distilled down into the simple idea, "a thousand songs in your pocket."

God and gave him an accurate understanding of his own need for forgiveness.

- ***We sense his calling.*** Some people push back on the idea of a definitive calling from God. But calling can take different forms. Not everyone has a "road to Damascus" experience like Paul. Some may experience more of a Nehemiah-style call which is confirmed through prayer, Scripture, and a strong compulsion to walk through an open door. As a newly married couple living in Jerusalem, Victoria and I had been praying for God to show us what was next. We had been married for less than a year and were seriously considering serving with Jews for Jesus. I had an open door to go but wanted to be confident it was where God wanted us to be, so I pursued God in prayer. I persisted until I was confident I knew it was his will; then I acted.
- ***We are ready to do what is necessary, even if that means putting ourselves at risk.*** Nehemiah decided to go to the king and prayed for favor. He knew the potential danger of communicating his situation to the king. Does your vision come at any potential cost to you? Serving God doesn't necessarily mean living in straw huts, but you will face obstacles. Nehemiah's challenges were only just starting. He would continue to experience opposition throughout the project. As soon as the work in Jerusalem was underway, Nehemiah and his team were attacked. Having a clear vision prepares us to face obstacles. Without one, we may abandon ship when things get hard.

If you are still unsure, keep in mind that God is faithful to redirect our vision if we seek him each step of the way. It's important to discern what God is laying on your heart and what's ultimately driving you, but don't assume you will always have total clarity.

Finally, before committing to any big project, the question "Why?" is essential. If you are going to invest yourself for months or even years in a mentally fatiguing project, you want to know you're not wasting your energy. Part of gaining a vision is being willing to explore what the need is and why a new ministry (or re-launch of an existing one) is necessary. I urge you to spend time with your current team in prayer and reflection around your vision. You need to seek a general answer to the "why" inspiring your vision. A few questions may be of value to you as you prayerfully begin to identify your vision:

- What is the big idea and how will it change people's lives? What could we accomplish together?
- Why is now the right time?
- What is God showing us?

Over time, God expanded the vision he gave Yoel, Karol, and me for how to best reach people in Jerusalem. We split our missionaries from all over the world into ten teams, each with a focus on reaching a specific community. Whether university students, artists, sports enthusiasts, or ultra-Orthodox men, these teams spent over a year getting to know the needs, values, and intricacies of their community in order to develop projects that centered around that community.

After a month of outreach in Jerusalem, not only did our teams not get shut down, but they had been able to meet and share the gospel with thousands of Israelis and lead dozens to faith in Jesus. Instead of seeing the gospel as an unavoidable issue and being chased down the streets or beaten, we were, for the most part, welcomed in Jerusalem. From the fruit of this vision, we were able to plant a long-term work that has continued to flourish in Jerusalem eight years later.

It was around that same season that the leadership of Jews for Jesus changed our mission statement to reflect this change in our evangelistic strategy. Today it states, "We relentlessly pursue God's plan for the salvation of the Jewish people." We were able to find our way forward in Jerusalem. But it all started with vision.

Vision is the first part of clarifying your mission. Next we will look at the importance of building a team to help bring that vision to life.

DISCUSSION QUESTIONS

- In your own words, what is your vision for your ministry?
- Where do you want to go?
- What do you hope to accomplish? How will your ministry change people's lives?
- Is it aligned with God's vision? What is God showing you?
- Why do you believe this is the right time?

SIX

LAUNCH STAGE PART 3

IDENTITY—WHO ARE WE?

BEFORE TAKEOFF, not only do we need a direction of where the mission is headed but we also need a crew to help us get there. Successful leaders understand that their vision doesn't begin and end with them. They invite others to dream about the possibilities and to imagine how they could help make that vision a reality. Maybe you already have a team fired up and ready to go. Or maybe you don't yet have anyone in mind! We will look at both working with an existing team and building a new team. But before we do so, it's important to grapple with what kind of leader you are.

Self-aware leaders know who they are and are aware of their abilities. But they are also aware of their limitations. They know they cannot do it alone and they need others.

Nehemiah knew who he was. He was a Jew living in forced exile, and a servant to the king. None of that said "leader." But his vision compelled him to act beyond the sphere of his own influence when he asked the king for permission to return to Jerusalem and rebuild. On his own, Nehemiah never would have been able to do what he believed God was asking him to do. When the king gave him a green light to go to Jerusalem, Nehemiah discovered others similarly burdened for Jerusalem. He shared his vision with "the Jews, the priests, the nobles, the officials, and the rest who were to do the work" (Nehemiah 2:16). Eventually he put together a team to make the vision a reality.

THE *I* IN TEAM

Nehemiah's example highlights the importance of both knowing who you are and identifying who you need. Before adding people to your team, it is important to take an unflinching inventory of who you are. Consider your talent and gifting, but also work to identify your heart motivations, character strengths, and weaknesses. Do you work well with others? Can you delegate responsibility? Are you sensitive to criticism? Are you resilient under stress? Do you tend to look at the big picture or see the details? Why do you want to launch this initiative? The answers to these kinds of questions will shape the kind of team you need—and this process shouldn't be rushed.

In Jewish thinking, the *lev,* or "heart" is the center of emotion and feeling, but it is also the center of our thought life. The *lev* is where our desires, thoughts, feelings, and fears all mix together and shape our inner self. The desires of the heart can be extremely complex and intertwined. To make matters more complicated, the heart is tainted by sin. Jeremiah wrote, "The heart is deceitful above all things, and desperately sick; who can understand it?" (Jeremiah 17:9) After Solomon ascended to the throne, God asked him what he desired. Solomon asked for *lev shomea,* a listening or understanding heart, so that he could discern wisdom and lead his people. Understanding what is going on inside—self-awareness—is crucial for leadership.

Daniel Goleman, author of *Emotional Intelligence*, argues EI is crucial for leadership success. "CEOs are hired for their intellect and business expertise—and fired for a lack of emotional intelligence." He concludes that self-awareness is "the keystone of emotional intelligence."[1] Stanford's Graduate Business Advisory Council surveyed seventy-five of its members, who agreed self-awareness was the most important capability for leaders to develop. "Executives need to know where their natural inclinations lie in order to boost them or compensate for them. Self-awareness is about identifying personal idiosyncrasies—the characteristics that executives take to be the norm but actually represent the exception."[2]

Unfortunately, self-awareness appears to be in short supply. In a study of seventeen thousand individuals from around the world, Hay Group Research discovered that 19 percent of female executives exhibited self-awareness in comparison to only 4 percent of their male counterparts. "Women often face barriers throughout their careers that require them to develop these skills to excel and advance in their organizations, in effect better preparing them for the challenges and complexities of leading in a dynamic business environment."[3]

Despite the fact that some people are naturally more self-aware than others, there are ways for every leader to develop greater self-awareness. Personality assessments like the Enneagram, the Myers-Briggs Type Indicator, StrengthsFinder, and Working Genius can be helpful tools to gain a deeper understanding of yourself. Additionally, StrengthsFinder and Working Genius emphasize the importance of having a mix of strengths and skills on a team. A good leader remembers that knowing yourself isn't simply about focusing on strengthening your own areas of weakness. It's about creating a team with others who have strengths you may be lacking.

If you are naturally inclined toward solving tactical questions you need to find others who can help you figure out the "Why?" questions. And if you naturally ask big questions, you need people who know how to implement ideas.

You can't do it all. Moses is an example of someone who lacked confidence as a public speaker. So God raised up his brother, Aaron, to speak for him. We are all going to be stronger in some areas than others. I know I am not administratively gifted and need to work closely with capable administrators if I want to develop and implement a vision. Some of us have strengths that come so naturally to us that we have trouble imagining others don't possess them too. My wife, Victoria, is amazing at staying in touch with people. We have friends we haven't seen in twenty years and Victoria reaches out regularly to stay in contact with each one. She sends cards for birthdays, presents when children are born, and calls them to catch up from time to time. She is such a natural that she's bewildered when others forget to stay in touch. But we aren't all wired like Victoria. We all have different strengths and weaknesses.

Years ago, I took a class on organizational psychology. We were asked to complete a 360-degree leadership assessment. The assessment was sent to our current and former colleagues to provide insight into our strengths and weaknesses as leaders. I received anonymous feedback from around fifteen current and former colleagues, including people I had managed, peers with whom I had worked, and current and previous supervisors. It was an extensive evaluation with dozens of questions. We then received our assessments in class. The teacher gave us a few minutes to privately read through the feedback. I still remember hearing the groans around the room. The unfiltered comments were unsettling.

I can't emphasize enough the importance of getting feedback. There is no substitute for receiving honest feedback from people you trust. This can come in many forms. Pastors, mentors, spiritual directors, peers, friends, and spouses can all be valuable as we look to develop and grow in our leadership. Executive coaching can also be a helpful way to learn more about yourself and grow as a leader.

Do what you can to make it easy for people around you to be honest and transparent with you. If you blast someone after they just plucked up the courage to let you know something about yourself, you will find yourself insulated from honest feedback as people hesitate to share with you in the future.

Finally, a word of caution: personality tests and leadership assessments can help you discover more about yourself, but don't let these tests, or even the feedback from others, determine the authorized version of you. I have heard people pigeonhole themselves with statements like, "Empathy isn't one of my strengths" or "I'm not creative." While it is important to know our strengths and weaknesses, it is possible to develop empathy and keep in mind that fantastic ideas often come from non-creatives. You are lots of things. There are many dimensions to who you are, and while you may not become great in a particular area of weakness, you may be amazed at how much you grow.

WORKING WITH AN EXISTING TEAM

Many leaders do not have the freedom to build a team entirely from scratch. They inherited staff, boards, elders, and stakeholders from a previous iteration of the organization. While this may feel challenging or even limiting, it can be an opportunity. It's important to point out that not all the people on your staff necessarily have to be involved with every aspect of your creative process. You may find several of your team members are enthusiastic and excited about the direction you want to go. That is a great start. Don't be too concerned if there are people who don't understand where you want to go. It's your responsibility to help them see, to paint a picture that helps them envision what could be. Sometimes the most unlikely collection of team members becomes a solid team that can work together to accomplish great things.

Before starting to look for new team members, consider the crew God has already put in your path. You may already have a team. There is an advantage to working with people with whom you have a track record. You've built a measure of trust and have experience working together.

Also, it's not always realistic to assume you can get rid of your current team. Many missions and churches have long-standing leadership teams or elders used to weighing in on decisions. That being said, if you hope to move forward, you will need to be honest if someone on your current team isn't a good fit.

BUILD A NEW TEAM

Whether you work with people you already know or search for new people to add to the mix, it is possible to build a functional, collaborative team. Organizations with strong teams have an advantage in today's complex, information-heavy landscape. Management expert Patrick Lencioni says, "Teams can achieve more than individuals could ever imagine doing alone."[4] Leadership thinking has evolved away from the idea of a lone-wolf, command-and-control style leader who does it all in favor of a collaborative, team-oriented approach. I believe that every leader needs a solid team to build and sustain a healthy, thriving ministry.

Reflect on your broader network of colleagues and friends. Think of leaders you have found helpful in the past. Pay attention to people in your circles who have similar vision or passion. It's possible they won't be able to officially join your team right away. Maybe you can't afford to hire them. That shouldn't be a deal-breaker. Moishe Rosen's first Jews for Jesus team was all volunteers. Tuvya Zaretsky, one of the founders, recalls, "Moishe couldn't employ me, but I was welcome to have meals at his house, [and] sleep on his floor. However, right in line with his priorities, he added 'All I have to offer you is an opportunity to serve the Lord.'"[5]

God used teams throughout history to accomplish his mission. Moses and Aaron, Caleb and Joshua, Paul and Barnabas. Jesus himself, the most effective ministry leader that ever existed, gathered twelve disciples who would build his church. He modeled the way we were meant to work together. That's why Paul described the church as parts of a body working together (1 Corinthians 12:12-27). Individually we are limited, but together we become dynamic.

One of the core values of Jews for Jesus is teamwork. We recognized that we do far better work when we work together. Not only are we able to see things more clearly because of the diversity of perspectives, but we can marshal a range of talents and expertise to accomplish far more than one of us could accomplish alone. And a team can support and encourage its members when the work is difficult.

Jews for Jesus had started as a team within the ABMJ mission. Known as the "Jews for Jesus experiment," this group of young, committed Jewish followers of Jesus was passionate about reaching other Jewish people with the gospel. Their concentrated, contextualized counterculture efforts to reach Jewish hippies saw immediate results. It wasn't long before they began to make a name for themselves. These Jews for Jesus made an eighteen-month commitment to serve together. Midway through that commitment, things took an unexpected turn as Moishe and his experiment were released from the ABMJ. Jews for Jesus would officially incorporate in 1973, but they were a new ministry that had lots of experience working together as a team.

Moishe wasn't from the demographic of these young hippies. Aware of his own limitations, he intentionally gathered younger Jewish people to serve alongside him. This illustrates an important principle: keep your key audience in mind as you form your team. You'll want to apply the same reflection you gave to your own strengths and weaknesses to your team. Assessing each member's strengths and weaknesses is an essential starting point, but it is of value to consider how the demographics of your team connect with the demographics of the people you're hoping to serve. Who are you already working with? Are you all men in your forties? Are you all from the same economic background? Did you all grow up in the church? What kind of training do you all have? Many people have a tendency to gravitate toward likeminded people. But Paul's body illustration should caution us from that. We don't want ten sets of eyes and no feet to help us get around.

An ideal team should be diverse in age, experience, gender, background, and education. This isn't simply for optics or to appear inclusive. A diverse team can help us see problems from different perspectives. When searching for answers to complex questions like, "Why are young families leaving our church?" or "Why have we not been able to connect with high school students?" we need to see the problem from different angles. It helps to have people from diverse backgrounds. For example, a group of single men are going to struggle to understand the challenges young mothers face. Adding a young mother to the team will provide valuable insight.

In addition, a well-rounded team can add much-needed expertise. I remember the first time I worked with a gifted administrative assistant. I felt liberated and my focus immediately sharpened. If you don't have someone that is good with logistics or finance, you will have a hard time getting your vision off the ground. A ministry looking to educate lay leaders through the launch of an online Bible school, for example, will benefit from having more than a group of Bible teachers on the team. Imagine what you could accomplish if you added an experienced web designer or a skilled marketer. It may seem obvious, but it's surprising how often this is overlooked.

Management expert Jim Collins noted how important it is for a leader to focus on team-building in his business classic *Good to Great: Why Some Companies Make the Leap and Others Don't*. "Getting the right people, in the right seats on the bus" is as true today as it has ever been.[6] Mission Design requires assembling a team with a range of talent that can see things from different perspectives.

Whether you build your team with staff or volunteers, each member should feel a sense of ownership and investment in the project to help you stay the course in the work God has called you to do.

WHAT IS AN IDEAL TEAM SIZE?

There isn't a one-size-fits-all team. It depends on many factors. What stage are you at? Are you kicking an idea around? Are you ready to launch? If so, what kind of program or ministry are you launching? The answer to your question will determine the kind of people you'll need. Most small projects start with two to three people and pick up partners along the way. When working on Massah, I reached out to Daniel Goldstein. He was a sharp go-getter with a proven track record. He was responsible, hardworking, and close in age to the people I was hoping to reach. Plus I knew he would complement my leadership style. I remember pitching the vision to him, and he was immediately interested. Together, the two of us were able to launch the project and add team members as it grew. The program continues to this day.

That doesn't mean there aren't better sized teams. In my experience, teams of three to six people seem to work best. When a team gets too much bigger it becomes unwieldy. It becomes more difficult to get consensus and decision-making can get bogged down. On the other hand, if your team is too small, you may struggle with insular thinking and a lack of expertise to get your vision off the ground.

HOW TO ASSEMBLE YOUR TEAM

Taking an inventory is an essential part of beginning to build a team. Start by making a list with two columns. On one side, write down what kind of person you need to get your vision off the ground; in the other column, who you currently have. In the "who you need" column, think about the kind of team members you need to help get your mission launched. Here are a few categories to consider:

Experts

- People with management experience
- Tech experts
- Creatives to help generate ideas
- Finance people

Diversity

- Ages
- Social and racial backgrounds
- Economic backgrounds
- Men and women
- Personality types
- Spiritual gifts

Passion for the cause

- People who believe
- People who primarily care about the mission
- People who support the mission financially and in other ways

Supportive

- Hard workers
- Committed to you
- Sounding boards
- Spiritually healthy
- Humble

As you assemble your team, keep in mind that the "Who are we?" question will affect the "Where are we going?" and the "Who are we serving?" questions, so it is important to be intentional about the people you invite to be part of your team.

DISCUSSION QUESTIONS

- What skills or traits do you have that help you in leading a team? What skills or traits might you be missing that would be helpful if others on the team had them?
- Who do you have on your current team? What are their special skills? Are there still skills that are missing in order to better serve the community you want to reach?

SEVEN

LAUNCH STAGE PART 4

PEOPLE—WHO DO WE SERVE?

MASSAH WAS A SOLUTION TO A PROBLEM. In 2006, we were trying to figure out how to capture the hearts and imaginations of Jewish Millennials. We had been running evangelistic programs for years but were seeing an alarming drop in interest and participation. The impact of this lack of engagement from the next generation meant the organization was effectively aging as younger staff were struggling to fit into our organization. It was clear it wouldn't simply be a matter of giving our existing programming a facelift. If we were going to engage Millennials, we were going to have to do something far more drastic.

Desperate to understand who these younger people were and why they felt the way they did, we immersed ourselves in their world. We spent time with Jewish Millennials. We read what they read. We sought out research and demographic studies. Jews for Jesus even commissioned a Barna study on Jewish Millennials.[1] But perhaps the most important thing we did was listen to them. We didn't realize it yet, but we had started to think like designers.

We knew we needed focus. Our vision was to raise up college-age Jewish young adults for ministry and service. If we hadn't narrowed our focus, we would have been building programs to serve young professionals, college students, and high schoolers all at the same time. Since each of these communities had such different needs, designing for all three would have been impractical. Without a focus on a key audience, we would have wasted precious time, money, and energy that we didn't have to spare. That focus emerged from prayer.

We prayerfully sought to discern what God was already doing in the community we hoped to reach. He had given us a burden for a specific group, and he had captured our attention as we sought to understand what this group was all about.

Even the most compelling vision shared by an incredible team of people has no real purpose if it doesn't put the people it hopes to serve at the center. Long gone are the days when a company would rely on the brilliance of a visionary CEO or creative team to develop a new product line that would be marketed to as many people as possible. In today's saturated market, a sea of products competes for our attention.

Today, people have become conditioned to personalized marketing. Companies increasingly rely on data and technology like AI to shape messaging and corporate strategy. The most successful companies strive to understand what customers care about before they know it themselves. They are willing to spend the necessary time and resources to make products and programs based on actual needs and interests. But those of us in ministry and in the nonprofit sector must continually seek to discover what our target audience needs and wants, and how to best connect our offerings with them right where they're at.

The proliferation of media channels and platforms makes connecting with the people you hope to reach even more challenging. Part of knowing your audience today means searching out and becoming adept at using the social media channels where they're active. If you hope to understand what they care about and how they prefer to communicate, you have to first know who they are.

Some years ago, our leadership team had the pleasure of working with Mike Volkema, former CEO of Herman Miller and current board chair of MillerKnoll. Throughout his tenure with

Herman Miller, Mike worked with some of the world's leading thinkers and designers. He explained that the difference-maker for organizations like MillerKnoll lies in their ability to design around the needs of their clients. He called it an outside-in approach as opposed to an inside-out approach. Rather than creating something their customers might want (inside-out thinking) they seek out regular input from their customers on what they actually need (outside-in thinking). They can then use that input to design more useful products and services to meet their clients' needs. But in order to do any of this, you have to know who your clients are.

The first broadside Moishe Rosen wrote and printed in the 1970s was called *A Message from Squares*. Unlike most other gospel tracts, it was filled with self-depreciating humor. He wrote it with a specific audience in mind. He wasn't trying to talk to rabbis or older Jewish immigrants. He was tuned in to young Jewish counterculture hippies, and he was trying to reach them with the good news. It proved to be an extremely effective communication tool to reach thousands of Jewish people with the gospel.

Decades later, our staff around the world were still handing out the same style of literature to everyone. Instead of creating dialed-in messaging that spoke to specific audiences the way Moishe had done, we were essentially trying to reach everyone the same way. It wasn't like we had intentionally decided not to focus on any particular key audience. It kind of just happened over the years. Sometimes organizations intentionally pivot away from one audience to another, but in our case, we just no longer had a clear focus of who we were meant to be reaching.

I remember talking about this with Mark Reynolds from City to City. He described something similar that happened to Redeemer Presbyterian Church in New York City. Early on, Tim Keller was focused on reaching skeptics and intellectuals with the gospel. Redeemer's programs were geared toward young professionals and college students. Each week thousands poured into the Hunter College auditorium. Mark pointed out that back then, a kids' you are cool because you want peace. we want Peace too but we're afraid to lay down the sword because It might not happen.

We both want LOVE but we settle for either sex or sermons.

We all want LIFE. Most get a kind of living death called existence...

We tried to be the Saviours of the world and we just end up sinning against those we want to save.

Maybe Jesus, the real Saviour, Can save us, give us Peace and help us come alive to Live and Love.

"For God so loved the world that he gave his only begotten son, that whosoever believes in him should not perish but have everlasting Life" John 3:16

JEWS FOR JESUS

Moishe Rosen
P.O. Box 545
Corte Madera, Ca. 92425
924-6677 or 479-4793

A MESSAGE FROM SQUARES

Hey You with The beard on your Face!

We think you are beautiful.

God likes beards too.

He didn't want the Israelites to even Trim their beards![1]

1. Lev. 19:27

You're Brave to do your own thing.

Most of us dont have the heart to make the scene.

Most of us are uptight. We're not satisfied with daily bread. we gather pots of Manna to last a whole lifetime, Like God was going to lose his Job and we were going to have to take care of ourselves.

You've got the Courage to be what you are in Front of The world.

Most of us prefer Secret sins so that we can keep up the Front. We're Lily whitewashed

when you're no place You take A Trip.

Most of us are no place— but we're there in Split-level Suburb style.

Maybe most everybody's Noplace.

Figure 7.1. "A Message from Squares" circa 1973

program wasn't even on their radar. Today Redeemer has a very different demographic and a huge program for kids.

If vision is a bit like your destination (Are we going to the moon or Mars?) and your team are a bit like your crew, the people you serve are the reason you go. The ones whose lives will be changed if you make the journey. The outcomes are extremely different depending on whom you're trying to serve. You want to be as specific as possible. If your church or ministry has a "we minister to whoever" model, then you run the risk of not orienting your programs to anyone in particular. You will end up being out of step with the needs of your constituency.

In the past few years, Jews for Jesus has shifted toward ministry to particular key audiences. Each of our global teams now focuses on serving at least one key audience. The goal is to understand who they are, what they care about, and how we can best reach them.

Tony Fadell, the engineer behind the development of the iPod, also founded Nest Thermostats. He described the impact people have on shaping a product. When Nest developed their home alarm system, they found that the men and women they interviewed had completely different needs. The men focused on security for their homes and possessions when they were away, while the women were primarily concerned for the safety of their children when they were at home. It is easy to imagine how design would be very different for each of these audiences.

Creating a profile or persona of the type of person you intend to serve will be helpful as you focus on addressing the needs of that specific group of people. Ultimately, the goal is to design programs that meet needs, and creating personas can help you do that more effectively. We will talk more about this in chapter eight.

When you focus on a key audience, a specific community to reach, you might not know much about them to begin with. Nevertheless, it's imperative to first have an idea of the people you are trying to reach as you begin to flesh out the mission and how you want to accomplish it. At Jews for Jesus, we built a workbook that each of our teams uses to learn more about their key audience to then develop further ministry. A modified version of the workbook has been provided in Appendix A for you to use with your team.

THE SWEET SPOT

Now that you have thought through your vision, your identity, and the people you serve, it's time to take a closer look at where they overlap to help you determine your mission.

Mission can be found at the intersection of your vision, your identity, and the needs of your key audience. Let's look at an example of an organization that has done this successfully.

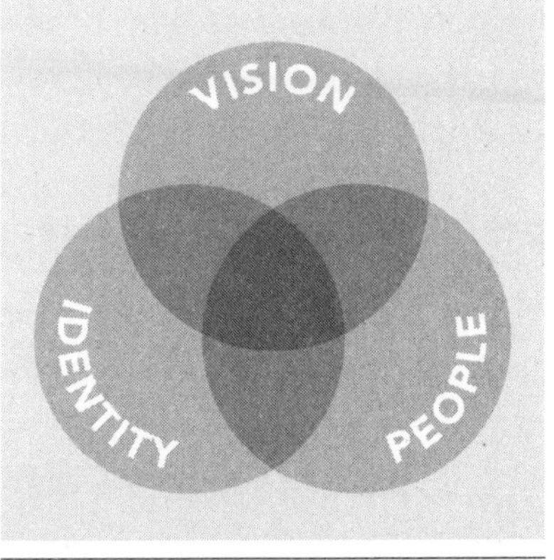

Figure 7.2. The intersection of vision, identity, and people

- ***Tearfund:*** Christian charity based in Teddington, UK; focuses on tackling extreme poverty.
- ***Their vision:*** To see people freed from poverty, living transformed lives, and fulfilling their God-given potential.
- ***Their identity:*** They are Christians embedded in churches around the world with a deep passion for helping people struggling with poverty. Many of their staff and leaders have lived and served in the poorest countries in the world.
- ***Their people:*** They serve people living in poverty in the fifty poorest countries in the world.
- ***Their mission:*** To follow Jesus where the need is greatest, responding to crises and partnering with local churches and organizations to help people lift themselves out of poverty.

Tearfund has a distinctive call that sets them apart from other relief organizations. They found their sweet spot. You too need an understanding of your vision, your identity, and the people for whom your organization exists. You may wish to frame an initial mission statement, but don't worry too much about refining it yet. This stage isn't about mapping out every detail. It's about figuring out which direction you and your team are headed. Try not to get stuck in this stage as you can always go back and fine-tune. You want to have a general idea of where you are headed so you can take the next step toward getting your mission off the ground. We will look at how to do this in the next chapter: the Explore Stage.

DISCUSSION QUESTIONS

- Describe the community or communities that you want to serve. What do you know about them? What do you want to know that you don't already?
- On a piece of paper or a whiteboard, draw your Venn diagram with the three circles: Vision, Identity, People. Write words or phrases that describe each circle. Where are the overlaps? What is your sweet spot?

EIGHT

EXPLORE STAGE

EMPATHIZE AND UNDERSTAND

RUSSIAN-SPEAKING JEWISH MINISTRY has been one of the most fruitful Jews for Jesus efforts to date. Since the late 1980s, we have seen God work powerfully in the lives of thousands of Russian-speaking Jewish people around the world. With the fall of the Soviet Union in 1989, an estimated 1.7 million Jews fled the USSR in search of better lives and new opportunities.[1] While the vast majority immigrated to Israel, many remained in Ukraine, Russia, and Belarus. Others settled in the United States, Canada, and Germany. In each of these places we discovered a people hungry for God's touch in their lives. This area of ministry continues to be tremendously fruitful. Since the Russian invasion into Ukraine in 2022, we have steadily seen God's hand at work in the lives of Ukrainian Jews, both in Ukraine and among those who relocated elsewhere.

A few years back, I met with our Russian-speaking ministry leaders to try to address a problem: the majority of people to whom they ministered were fifty and older. Grateful as we were for the incredible ministry we had to older Jewish people, we longed to expand our ministry to the next generation.

I asked our leaders in Russia, Ukraine, and Belarus for a list of Jewish young adults to interview. The list had thirteen names. We created a questionnaire including questions like, "What kind of

Jewish activities do you do?" "What is the most important thing to you about being Jewish?" "How would you describe your beliefs?" and "What do you think about Jews for Jesus?" The point of the interview wasn't to just get through the questionnaire but to listen and to ask follow-up questions. I asked them to keep notes of their interviews, and to focus on listening and observing. To pay attention to body language. When did they get more animated? When did they seem to close up? What topics did they want to discuss more? What seemed to stand out from the conversation? The goal was to understand and empathize with these young adults.

The Explore Stage is all about observing and listening to our key audience so we can better understand them and design with their needs in mind. Picture our rocket ship. It has cleared the atmosphere and is now orbiting earth. From here the crew is positioned to see everything. They now have the best view of the planet. This stage of the Mission Design process is to take a broad view and take everything in. It is premature at this stage to settle on solutions or draw conclusions. The goal is to gather information and glean specific insights while broadening our perspective as we seek to understand our key audience.

Here is a road map through the Explore Stage:

Empathy leads to . . .

Better Observation leads to . . .

Meaningful Insights lead to . . .

Identifying Real Needs leads to . . .

New Opportunities lead to . . .

Better Design

At the heart of good Mission Design is empathy. Empathy is a posture or mindset required of every team member in order to move forward. To get a deeper understanding of what empathy is and how it can help your design process, let's take a look at an approach rooted in empathy: Design Thinking.

DESIGN THINKING

There is a plethora of human-centered design tools that can be useful in ministry, including Service Design, Experience Design, Product Design, Customer Design, UI, UX, Agile, Lean, and Scrum. While the array of options can be a little overwhelming, I have found Design Thinking to be a powerful starting point for Mission Design. Design Thinking is a process that can help companies and organizations find solutions to complex human problems.

The origins of Design Thinking can be traced back to architecture, industrial design, and product design from the 1960s, but its application to business and organizational solutions was popularized in the 1970s and '80s by the design consultancy Ideo. Ideo incorporates design principles into an interdisciplinary problem-solving approach that puts people at the center. Behind the scenes, Ideo has been involved in numerous breakthrough products, including the Apple mouse, the Nest thermostat, and the Fitbit. Over the past decade or so, Ideo has focused more on service-related and public-sector challenges. They partnered on projects like Bill and Melinda Gates Foundation's Teachers Know Best education platform and Bank of America's Keep the Change initiative. Today, Design Thinking has become commonplace in many industries.

A quick glance around the internet will show different Design Thinking charts, but here are the basic steps:[2]

1. ***Empathize:*** This stage is all about cultivating a mindset focused on people. Through observing and listening, you begin to understand your key audience and their needs.
2. ***Define:*** What insights and opportunities did you discover? This stage is all about making sense of your findings, looking for patterns, and telling stories.
3. ***Ideate:*** Take those insights and opportunities you discovered and begin to generate ideas and potential solutions. This is

where you get as creative as possible. Brainstorm ideas; get them all out there. Zero in on areas of opportunity.

4. ***Prototype:*** Take the best ideas from the previous stage and try them out. A prototype is meant to be quick and cheap. The idea is that it can fail without too much commitment of time or resources.
5. ***Test:*** Get feedback from the people you serve. Did it work? How could it be improved?

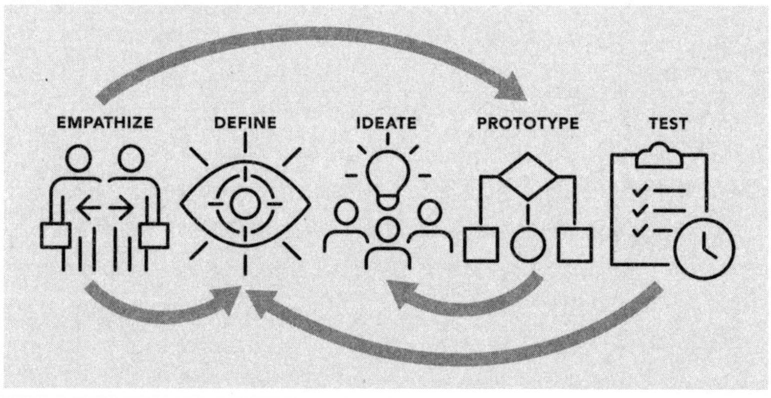

Figure 8.1. Design thinking: a five-stage, sometimes nonlinear, process

The team repeats some or all of these steps as necessary.

Design Thinking does not begin with programs or big plans. In today's saturated market, companies and organizations cannot afford to waste time launching another app or service without knowing whether there is a need for it. Design Thinking starts with people and what they actually want and need. It requires a deep understanding of the community for whom you're creating by becoming a student of what they care about. This process begins with empathy.

EMPATHY

Perhaps the best way to describe empathy is by telling a story. It was a blistering hot summer day in New York, and I was weaving my way through the crowded streets of midtown to get to a meeting.

The streets were teeming with activity; shoppers, dog walkers, buskers, students, tourists—thousands of people determined to get where they were going. I briskly passed a group of tourists, when out of nowhere, a young man stepped in front of me wearing a turquoise smock and a big grin.

"Do you vote?" he asked me, clipboard in hand.

A little startled, I muttered, "Sorry, in a rush," and cut around him. I looked both ways and darted across the street toward the subway station. As I arrived at the entryway of the station, I was stopped again by a person wearing an identical blue smock and grin. He stood right in front of me and asked, "Do you vote?"

Suppressing irritation, I said, "Not now" and tried to push around him.

He danced in front of me again. "Why not now?" he asked.

The exchange was making me angry. I gave him a withering look and said, "Move!" then shot past him down the stairs to the subway. As I made my way down, I pondered my own frustration at the encounter. After all, what had he done wrong?

Then it dawned on me. I've been that guy. I had sent my team out in coordinated T-shirts to the busiest places in the city to hand out gospel tracts and to engage people on the streets. I like to believe I wasn't aggressive like that guy, but who knows? Maybe I had been perceived that way. Anger had been a common response from most of the people we encountered, and my assumption had been that they were angry with Jesus. While that may have been true for some, my experience that day made me see things differently. Being in the shoes of someone who had been confronted with an unwanted conversation on a hot day in crowded midtown provided fresh insight. Suddenly I was feeling what the people we'd approached with our tracts were feeling.

That kind of experience can be the beginning of empathy.

Empathy isn't just good for design. As Christians, we are called to empathize with others. In Galatians 6:2, Paul wrote, "Bear one another's burdens, and so fulfill the law of Christ." How can we care for one another without taking the time to understand or really see one another? Jesus himself demonstrated empathy by coming down to earth and being born into a Jewish home that existed in a land ruled by Rome. He gave up his kingdom reputation to relate to his chosen people—his key audience. Jesus didn't need to be near us in order to understand the deep-felt needs of his people. After all, he had a complete grasp of the human heart. Nevertheless, he drew close to us in order to demonstrate his deep love and compassion for us.

It's clear that empathy comes more naturally for some than for others. Fortunately, there are some useful tools to help every one of us grow in this area.

PRAYER

Yoel and Adel had been part of the Orthodox Jewish community in Jerusalem. Neither had found the answers there that they were looking for, so together they began searching. In 2001, through supernatural experiences, they were being drawn to Jesus. Together they were convinced he was the promised Jewish Messiah. They were baptized and joined our mission three years later.

Fast-forward to 2017. Jews for Jesus was planning to launch a new branch in Jerusalem. Our Israel director, Dan Sered, met with Yoel and asked him to pray about leading this new work. Yoel did pray about it, but he wasn't convinced he was the right person for the job. He had experienced a leadership failure abroad five years earlier and was still wrestling with his sense of calling. He didn't want to revisit past mistakes. To make matters more complicated, Yoel and his family were already settled in Jaffa, where they were helping to plant a church.

That same year, Yoel was asked to lead our first large-scale evangelistic outreach in Jerusalem. In his early conversations with Dan about launching the new branch, Yoel gave off strong "Jonah vibes." Just as the prophet had tried to flee from God's calling, Yoel admitted that this wasn't an assignment he welcomed. When the time came to lead the outreach in Jerusalem several months later, Yoel asked me to pray for him. I said, "How about this? You pray for me, and I'll pray for you." And so we began praying for each other.

Over time, his heart began to change. He agreed to relocate to Jerusalem with his family, taking on a supporting role under a younger leader. As they served together, Yoel started to see how he might step back into leadership. It was clear that God was working in his heart. When the younger leader had to leave the country due to visa issues, it became an answer to many prayers: Yoel realized that he was, in fact, the right person for the job. Many of his coworkers had believed he was a great fit all along. It was remarkable to witness how God had transformed his heart. Yoel has now been leading the ministry in Jerusalem for years and continues to grow in his vision for this important city.

Prayer isn't a tool to get God to give us this or to do that. It's about us finding alignment with what God is already doing. When we tap into that, not only are we transformed, but we are positioned to see God do what only he can do—and participate with him in that work.

GET OUT THERE

This discussion about change will reside in the category of theory until you are able to sit where your audience sits and see things from their perspective. This is easier said than done. Our life rhythms can get in the way. Many of us spend the vast majority of our time at home, at the office, in the car, dropping kids off at school or sports, and at church on the weekend. We spend 90 percent of our time surrounded by likeminded people. But to shift to seeking how to connect with others requires us to get close enough to figure out what they think about, what they care about, and what they need. It's a huge challenge. That is where immersion can help us break out of our bubble and draw close to the people we sense we're being called to serve.

Immersion has been Jews for Jesus' secret weapon. We integrated it into our regular ministry approach a number of years ago. Our mission staff seek to immerse themselves in the community and to participate in Jewish life. This can look different depending on the specific community and context. Immersion might be attending a Shabbat dinner for students, taking a Hebrew class, or participating in Jewish Community Center events. It might be joining a Jewish meetup, enrolling in a Jewish history class, or volunteering for a local Jewish cause. Immersion is about spending time with the people you are trying to reach. The idea is simple, but it requires intentionality and consistency.

Some go to even greater lengths to experience the world from the perspective of their key audience. A group of students from New York University was trying to solve the problem of how to help elderly New Yorkers safely get around the city streets. In order to understand what it felt like for an elderly person to navigate New York, the entire team dressed as elderly people with outfits, wigs, and glasses. They used walkers to get around, slowly and deliberately climbing stairs to the subway. It wasn't long before people grew impatient and started making comments while rushing around them. Turns out, New York was not built with the elderly in mind. The best way to grasp the challenges they experienced navigating the city was to step into the shoes of the people they were trying to help.

Look for opportunities to get out there and experience the world as your key audience does, and encourage your team to do the same.

OBSERVE AND LISTEN

Ministers need skills like preaching, teaching, and pastoring, but it's just as important for them to be able to observe and listen well. These often-neglected skills can yield significant benefits. This essential step can feel unproductive in the face of everything else we have to do, but it is essential to the design process. The good news is that paying attention and tuning in are muscles you can strengthen.

I encountered severe culture shock when I first moved from Seattle to Israel. Since I didn't speak Hebrew yet, I spent a lot of time listening. There were plenty of differences between Israeli and American culture, but the first thing I noticed was that Israelis were far more direct than I was used to. They would say what they meant. They would argue, even yell at one another. Then they would go get coffee together. In the US, this behavior would be interpreted as aggressive, even combative. But as I became familiar with Israeli culture, I understood that directness could be a sign of trust—even affection. There is a lot we can learn if we watch and listen.

Sometimes people tell you what you need to hear. I once took a class on nonprofit communications. After class I approached the professor, a Jewish woman who grew up in New York City. I asked how familiar she was with Jews for Jesus and what she thought about our brand. She shared generally about communications and branding. But after around ten minutes she looked at me and said, "Aaron, let me level with you. I think Jews for Jesus has the shittiest brand in the Jewish community." She had my attention.

"Why do you say that?" I asked.

She continued, "Look, I'm Jewish and grew up in New York. I encountered Jews for Jesus over the years and . . . Jesus shmeezus. I don't have an issue with Jesus, but you guys were always in my way." I could have debated with her or written off her comments as being biased, but that would have been a mistake. Her feedback was valuable; it gave us an honest window into how our key audience viewed our organization and its outreach efforts. We need to hear unfiltered feedback without feeling the need to defend ourselves or write it off.

It's important to observe nonverbal cues. Body language, eye contact (or lack thereof), and tone of voice can tell us a lot about people. Renowned behavioral psychologist Dr. Albert Mehrabian popularized his 7-38-55 percent rule.[3] The conclusion of his research was that roughly 7 percent of what is communicated is verbal communication or spoken words, while 38 percent and 55 percent were communicated through tone of voice and body language, respectively. That means, according to Dr. Mehrabian, 93 percent of communication is nonverbal! Imagine what we miss if we rely primarily on phone calls and email to communicate.

When we spent time interviewing Russian Jewish young adults, we received important information about what mattered to them through their nonverbal cues. We all noticed that the people we interviewed became visibly animated when the subject of Israel came up. We would have missed that if we relied solely on texts or emails to gather information.

Really listening to someone else in today's distracted world can make a big impression. If you are easily distracted, just making eye contact can require effort. One way to improve your listening skills is through the process of active listening. Active listening is used by counselors, therapists, and many others to fully understand what is being communicated by another person. This involves being fully present in the conversation, paying attention to body language, asking open-ended questions, and summarizing or reflecting back what you have heard to confirm you have properly understood what the other person is saying. *Harvard Business Review* has a great page on active listening and techniques on how to practice it—including understanding your default listening style and making an active, conscious choice on how to best listen.[4]

Getting to know and care for the people you are trying to reach is absolutely crucial to effectively communicating with them and serving them. It might sound cliché, but the old adage "Don't judge a man until you've walked a mile in his shoes" seems apt. How can we reach people we don't understand? In order to help you gain insight into your community, here are three tools I have found the most helpful: empathy maps, personas, and journey maps.

Empathy maps. Empathy maps help us understand what's happening above and below the surface, synthesizing observations and revealing deeper insights about a person's needs. They start with observing people's behavior—the externals of what they say and do. But they also attempt to understand people's attitudes—how they think and feel. Once again, this means getting out and interacting with people. Campus ministries like InterVarsity often scout out a new campus by physically walking the grounds and meeting new people from various spheres. Empathy maps require face time with the people you are trying to reach in order to understand what they really think and feel.

Of course, understanding what is going on inside someone else's head isn't simple.

For example, workers at a food pantry might map how the people they serve experience their food distribution. It's essential to pay close attention to how people interact, what they say, what they look at, and their body language. Sometimes it's possible to infer or guess what a person is thinking. Are they exhibiting signs of impatience, such as fidgeting, tapping their foot, or mumbling their frustration? Do they seem embarrassed to be there? How would that look different from impatience? Other times, the clients may verbalize exactly what they're thinking. A person might tell you they are confused by saying something like, "Is this where I should stand?" The point of the exercise is to attempt to understand more fully what it might be like to be in their shoes. There are plenty of good examples of empathy maps out there. Here are a few:

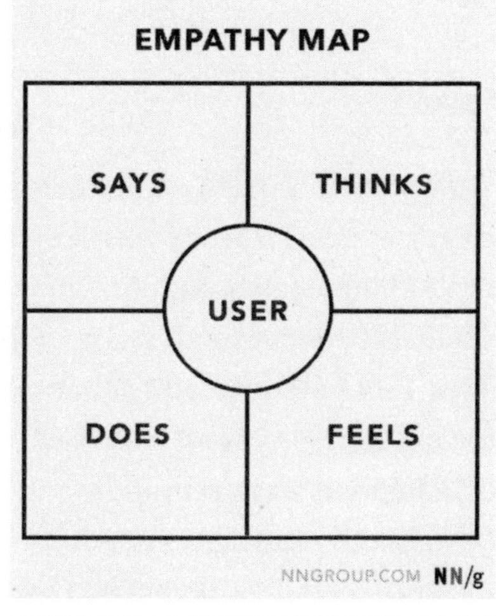

Figure 8.2. Empathy map—style one[5]

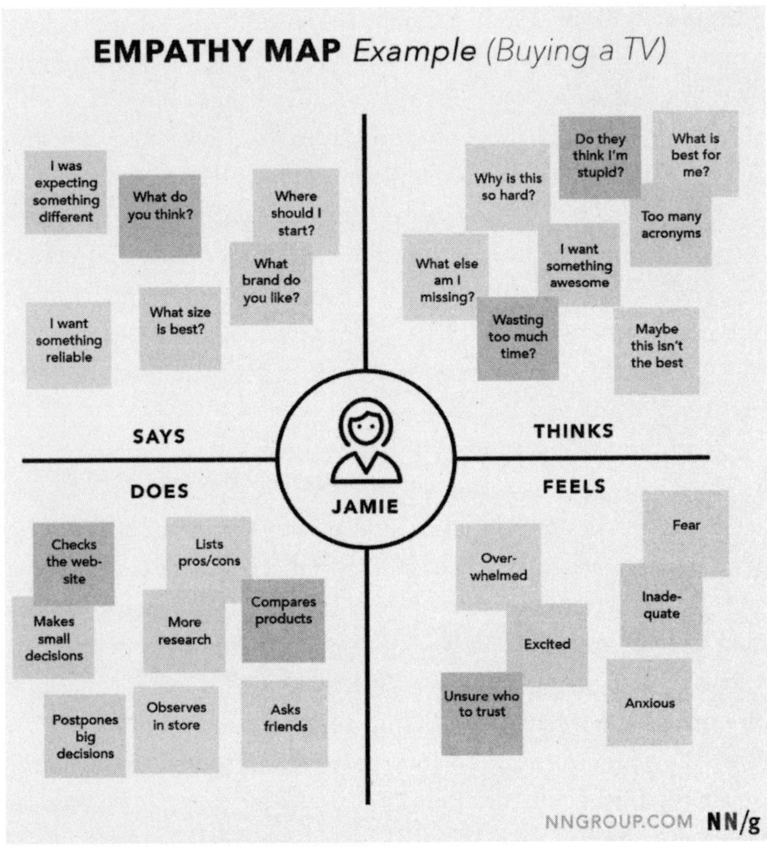

Figure 8.3. Empathy map—buying a TV[6]

Personas. A persona is a fictional yet realistic representation of a typical person from your key audience. Personas help create a three-dimensional picture. They could include a bio, work responsibilities, educational background, goals, and pain points. What does this person read? What do they watch? Which social platforms do they prefer? Hobbies?

When we were rebranding in New York, we had a number of Jewish communities in mind. To make it more tangible for our staff, we wrote personas for each of these groups. One of these personas was a man we named Jerry, an older Jewish Boomer from the

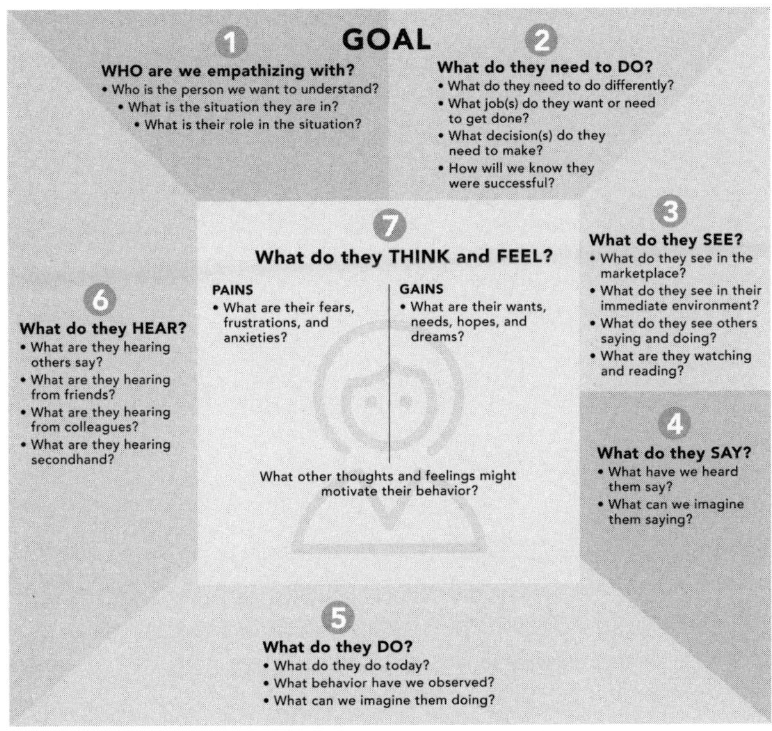

Figure 8.4. Empathy map—style two[7]

Upper West Side of New York—think of a personality like comedian Larry David. Our fictional Jerry was secular, affluent, direct, and a bit cynical, especially about Jesus. While personas should not be an actual person, they should be based on real people so you have an accurate representation of your key audience.

Journey maps. Journey maps (or customer journey maps) can be used to track each touchpoint a person will have as they interact with your services and experience your ministry. This tool is especially useful when you want to visualize how people engage with your organization. Where did they first find you? With whom did they interact? How did each of those interactions take place? In person? Via email? This map will capture each step they took along the way to receiving your services. The goal of this map is to try to capture their emotional state at each touchpoint throughout their experience. If you don't have an actual person in mind for your journey map, creating a persona can be helpful for this exercise as you map how someone from a key audience would interact with your organization. Table 8.1 is a sample journey map.

Table 8.1. Sample journey map of "Intermarried Margaret" and "Jewish Jerry"

Discover	Explore	Connect	Introduce	Coach
1. Margaret Googles "intermarriage" on her phone and finds JewishGentile-Couples.com. She is uncertain where to go.	**3.** She clicks the ad on her phone and reads the PDF. She is interested in finding out more.	**6.** Margaret responds to the Contact Us link on the website and sends an email.	**9.** Margaret lets Jerry know she wants them both to meet with Rob on Zoom. Margaret is feeling hopeful. Jerry is feeling uncertain.	**12.** Margaret, Jerry, and Rob meet on Zoom for their first coaching session. Rob listens and makes suggestions on next steps. He walks them through other various resources.
2. She sees our Facebook ad the next day inviting her to download our content offer: "20 tips for interfaith couples"	**4.** She explores our website on her laptop, reading about us and watching testimony videos. She finds the spiritual focus refreshing and is looking forward to finding out more. She is feeling hopeful.	**7.** Rob receives the notification and shoots Margaret an email that same day asking Margaret to share a bit more about her situation. He lets her know he would be open to a video chat if she is interested.	**10.** They decide to give it a shot and let Rob know via email they are both ready to meet.	**13.** Margaret and Jerry both agree to a second session. Jerry begins to listen to the podcast as well.
	5. She downloads and listens to episodes of the *Jewish Gentile Couples* podcast.	**8.** Margaret emails Rob, letting him know more about her and Jerry's situation and tells him she is interested in setting up a meeting.	**11.** Rob sets up a Zoom meeting with them both.	**14.** After six sessions, Margaret and Jerry are taking huge strides, and Jerry is now meeting with Rob one-on-one around faith issues.

"Intermarried Margaret" is a non-Jewish Christian married to "Jewish Jerry." Margaret and Jerry have struggled to understand one another, and their relationship has suffered over the past six months. Looking for help, Margaret discovers JewishGentile-Couples.com. This ministry was developed to help people like Margaret find both cultural and spiritual harmony with their partners.

You can see each point of interaction laid out chronologically. This can give your team a new way to look at the process and address the gaps or weakest links in the journey. Nielsen Norman Group and Service Design Tools are two resources that provide good templates to help you create journey maps for your key audiences.[8]

ADOPT AN OPEN, CURIOUS MINDSET

It can be difficult to see things from a different perspective. Our minds are quick to judge responses and behaviors. But if we truly want to understand how others see things, we need to stop and ask, "Why?" A curious and open posture is important if we are going to get beyond our own biases and presuppositions.

When we moved to Israel, I became close friends with an Israeli who had been raised in a settlement in the West Bank. His family were all strong Zionists and had served in the Israel Defense Forces. Yet what I remember most about him was how sympathetic he was toward Palestinians. He had personally experienced the conflict of the intifada, and yet he had a nuanced understanding of how complicated things were for people on both sides of the conflict.

Today, I marvel at how open and curious he was as a teenager! One mark of his influence in my life today is that I find it strange when I meet people who have never been to Israel yet have extreme, rigid views of the Middle East conflict. We need to work against our human tendency to assume we have it all figured out. If we close ourselves off to hearing others (even people with whom we may not see eye to eye), we will have a lopsided view of the world that can lead to misunderstanding, bias, and prejudice.

TRACK IMPRESSIONS AND INSIGHTS

You need to keep track of any insights that stand out to you. Keep notes on your interactions. Capture comments, questions, or even a look someone gave you. That means carrying a pen and paper around. Don't forget to ask your team to do the same so that you can track and discuss your findings later. Keep an eye out for patterns or similar responses you receive from interacting with your key audience. You will revisit these insights later when you enter the Design Stage.

Finally, remember that the Understanding Stage of Mission Design requires time and attention. It means spending lots of time with people. For those extroverts out there, this will come naturally. You may love every moment of being out there exploring who people are and what they care about. For others it may feel more draining. At times you may feel like you are diverting precious time to simply hang out with people. That is why having a diverse team is so important. Regardless, if you really want to understand who your constituents are and design for their actual needs you have to be able to observe and listen to them. There are no shortcuts here. Empathy is your best tool to get beneath the surface and to understand how others feel and what they care about.

After the team in Ukraine, Belarus, and Russia completed their interviews with the young adults, we reconvened to discuss what we had learned. As each leader shared about their experience, an insight began to emerge. These young adults were actively engaged with the subject of Israel. Many expressed an interest in traveling to Israel and even learning Hebrew. They spoke of family members and friends who had immigrated to Israel over the years, and some had even considered relocating themselves. It was no surprise. After all, Jewish culture had been suppressed for many years in the Soviet Union and they were hungry for more. We now understood they were fascinated with Israel, and they were interested in exploring their Jewish identity.

This process helped us get a better understanding of the needs of these young adults. We were then able to use these insights as we incorporated them into our ministry.

In the next stage, we will explore how to translate your insights into ideas.

DISCUSSION QUESTIONS

- Spend time observing and interacting with your key audience. Build an empathy map that describes how they see, hear, speak, and think about the world around them. (I highly recommend that you and your team work through the first two parts of Appendix A in order to get a better grasp of your key audience.)
- What are the needs of your community? What do they *think* they need to thrive?
- Pray for your key audience—for God to give you his heart for them and insights about how to best reach them for his kingdom.

NINE

REENTRY STAGE

DESIGN AND DEVELOP

MY TEAM HAD DECADES of collective ministry experience in New York City, yet understanding exactly how Jewish New Yorkers perceived Jews for Jesus wasn't an overnight process for us. Jews for Jesus has always been a results-oriented mission. We tracked things like the number of broadsides we handed out, the number of new contacts we received, and the number of people who made decisions to follow Jesus. It was clear we were seeing a steady decrease in the number of people we were ministering to. So we paused outreaches but didn't completely stop activity. We spent as much time as possible immersed in the community, talking with as many Jewish people as possible. We were doing our best to put our feet in the shoes of the people we hoped to reach.

While we longed to reach all two million Jewish New Yorkers with the good news of Messiah, we realized that we would need to narrow our focus if we hoped to reach anyone at all. The number of subgroups in the Jewish community was dizzying: Orthodox, Reform, students, unaffiliated, intermarried, artists, Israelis, just to name a few. We decided to focus on Jewish students and Jewish creatives as we already had a young, creative team that often connected with university students in Greenwich Village near NYU.

This meant getting out and becoming a part of these specific Jewish communities. We immersed ourselves in the art world. We spent time on the campuses. I enrolled in classes at NYU. I met Jewish thought leaders, including Reform rabbis, leaders of Hillel (a Jewish campus organization), Orthodox educators, a former ultra-Orthodox Jewish woman, and at least one convert to Judaism. One Jewish professor was initially wary of my involvement since I had informed him that I was the local Jews for Jesus director. Eventually he warmed to my presence and would even ask for my "Jews for Jesus perspective" in class from time to time. I received tons of unsolicited feedback. Classmates, teachers, even a few visiting lecturers didn't hold back. Some questioned my Jewish bona fides, others asked if I was there to proselytize, and others had no idea what to think. It was a gold mine of unfiltered insights into how different Jewish people felt about Jews for Jesus.

As our team spent time out and about engaging with people and experiencing Jewish life, a picture began to emerge. We discovered three important insights:

- ***Many people either had a distorted idea of Jews for Jesus or had no familiarity with the organization at all.*** We were used to people assuming all sorts of weird stuff about us. I had heard it all: We were Southern Baptists dressed up as Jews. We were a cult. We were paid per convert. We lured and baptized children. (Jews for Jesus has always had a strict policy that we not talk to people under eighteen years old without written consent from their parents or guardians.) The list of crazy ideas about our organization went on and on. People were often surprised to hear that our staffers grew up in Jewish families and hadn't been brainwashed but thoughtfully came to the conclusion that Jesus was the Messiah. But what surprised me most was how many students didn't know anything about us at all.
- ***Our particular brand of street evangelism was being interpreted as cultish behavior.*** Those who had seen our visible mass evangelistic

campaigns in New York each July had often also heard responses by Jewish antimissionary groups. They spent years painting us as a kind of cult like NXIVM or Scientology. As we fanned out in matching T-shirts to hand out literature throughout the subways, we were inadvertently reinforcing that stereotype.

- ***There was increasing admiration and interest in Jesus as a Jewish leader.*** There were more and more Jewish scholars reclaiming Jesus and his teachings. Orthodox Jewish scholar Amy Jill Levine published the Jewish Annotated New Testament. It was clear that there was Jewish interest in Jesus both as a humanitarian figure and as a Jew. It seemed there were new opportunities for dialogue about Jesus as a Jewish teacher.

As we pondered these insights, we recognized that they presented some unique opportunities. It was time to decide which of these opportunities to pursue.

BACK TO EARTH

The rocket illustration from figure 3.1 highlights the process of Mission Design. To review: In the Launch Stage, we focused on discovering our mission at the nexus of our vision, our team, and the needs of our key audience. In the Explore Stage, the rocket reached its cruising altitude. From that vantage point, the team had the best view from which to observe, learn, and gain insights about the people they serve.

The goal of the Reentry or Design Stage is to make sense of what we have discovered so we can bring it back to earth. In the Design Stage, we make sense of the insights and observations we've collected, and we brainstorm possible solutions that can meet the needs of our key audiences.

THE DESIGN APPROACH

Design Thinking draws its inspiration from broader principles in design. Prior to the 1960s, the concept of design was associated with visual arts, illustration, and fashion.[1] But in the decades since, design has been integrated into virtually every sector, including graphic design, software design, service design, interior design, industrial design, engineering design, and information design, to name just a few.

Famed architect and furniture designer Charles Eames defined design as "a plan for arranging elements in such a way as best to accomplish a particular purpose."[2] That description could apply to many areas of human life. Mission Design applies the principles and processes of design to create meaningful, impactful ministries. Design isn't simply about making objects look more appealing or helping them become more useful. Design helps us look deeper than programming and aesthetics toward relevant, consequential service to the community to which God is calling us.

There are lots of ways to talk about the design process, but figure 9.1 is one way to visualize it.

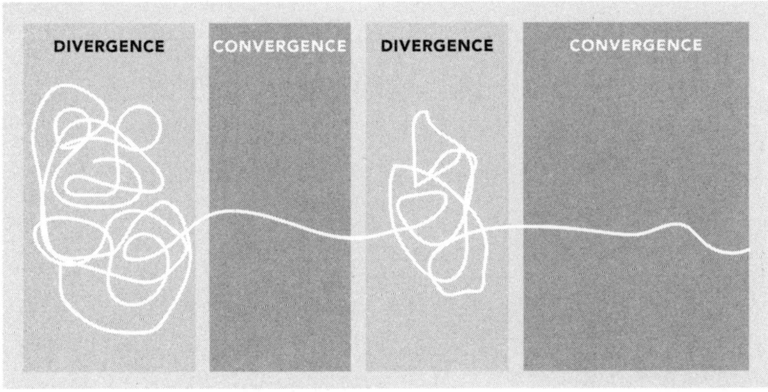

Figure 9.1. The design process—one view

Design isn't a linear process. We start out almost entirely with questions and move toward deeper knowledge of the people we are designing for.

Figure 9.2 is another way to look at it: we zoom out in order to discover, learn, and gain insights. Once we have a deeper understanding of our audience, we can identify opportunities that can

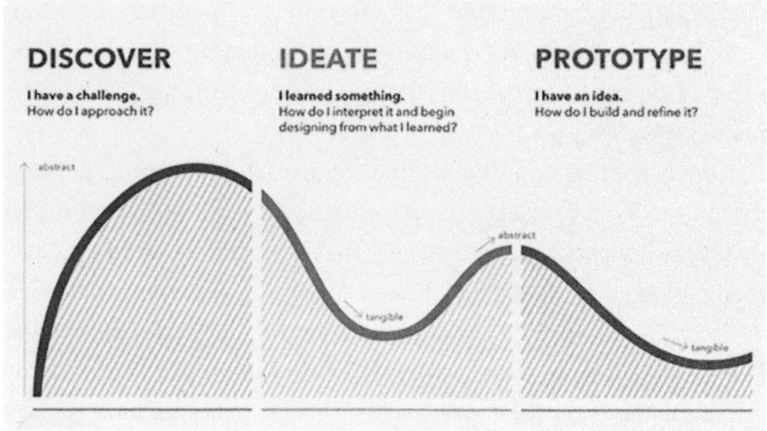

Figure 9.2. The design process—another view[3]

help us develop relevant, effective solutions. This is a crucial part of the process. But even after we begin to identify potential solutions, the creative process zooms back out again as we receive feedback so that we can recalibrate where necessary. This process creates a kind of loop where we test out ideas, get feedback, and refine our approach.

Figure 9.3 is another way to look at this process: the Build-Measure-Learn feedback loop is a powerful way to improve our design over time. Most design approaches have an iterative element to them. Just when you think you figured it out, expect to go back to the drawing board. This is an important part of the design process. You test out ideas and look for feedback. Did the program connect with your key audience? Did the idea meet a need?

Figure 9.3. The design process—continuous view

Rapid prototyping and evaluation can help us determine

whether an idea is a winner or a loser, and can help us determine whether we should persevere with one idea or pivot to another. In either case, the point is to be willing to stay in learning mode so we can adjust course and try again. The design approach enables us to iterate quickly without spending too much time or resources on bad ideas.

We will take a closer look at the value of getting feedback when we discuss prototyping and iteration in chapter eleven.

MAKE SENSE OF YOUR FINDINGS

It's now time to distill your findings into key insights and to identify good opportunities. As you and your team process what you are learning together, be careful not to jump to conclusions. Take time to discuss and reflect on what you have discovered. Early in my ministry with Jews for Jesus, I encountered many angry and openly hostile Jewish people as I went out on the streets and shared the gospel. During our evangelistic street campaigns, it wasn't uncommon to hear comments like, "Only an idiot would believe in Jesus," "You aren't Jewish," or "You're part of a cult."

As the years went on, I continued to interpret the hostility I encountered through my ministry with Jews for Jesus as disdain toward Jesus. As reasonable as that assumption may have been, it didn't square with my findings when I changed my approach. As our team began to experiment with a less "in your face" approach to sharing the gospel with Jewish New Yorkers, we discovered a more nuanced picture of what was going on. We found many were curious or at least neutral in their attitudes toward Jesus. I began to suspect that the reaction we experienced from some was more related to our brand and our approach than to anything they knew about Jesus. The only way to really know for sure was to test and get further feedback from our key audience.

Good design means we need to let go of assumptions. Even if we have been on the field for thirty years, it's important to continue to stay curious.

IDENTIFYING OPPORTUNITIES

In order to process what you have discovered with your team, each team member should bring their notes, quotes, pictures, empathy maps, and anything else they've discovered that may shed light on your key audience.

Our team noticed how people were responding to us, what kind of people were interacting with us, and who wasn't interacting with us at all. Through observing behavior and receiving actual feedback from our key audience, insights began to emerge. We brought those insights back and discussed them together. We noticed that each insight presented challenges but also revealed opportunities. When we realized that most Jewish people had a distorted idea of Jews for Jesus, we may have felt personally disappointed, but we also recognized this finding offered us an opportunity. We had a hypothesis: if we could change our approach and create space to get close enough to present ourselves as reasonable Jewish people with authentic Jewish experiences, we were confident this would create more nuanced personal impressions of Jews for Jesus and break negative stereotypes.

As you dig deeper and gain insights into how people feel, opportunities might be staring you in the face. These opportunities can lead to design solutions that can make a difference in the lives of your community. You will not be able to act on every opportunity due to the size or expertise of your team. You will want to take time with your team to discuss your discoveries. What are the most pressing needs? If you could only address one or two, what would they be? Consider which ones your team is best positioned to address and make a plan.

ASK BETTER QUESTIONS

Asking the right questions can clarify the scope and direction of your design challenge. Take the example I presented of Russian-speaking Jewish young adults in chapter eight. We were struggling to connect with the next generation, let alone minister to them. We discovered through our interviews that each one was interested in what it means to be Jewish and how Israel fits into that picture. As the team gained more insights, they were now able to better frame a design question. Something like, "How might we provide meaningful Jewish experiences that address the spiritual needs of the next generation of Russian-speaking Jewish young adults?"

Awana is a good example of an organization that has learned to ask questions. In the 1940s, Awana started as a kids' club in Chicago connected with a local church. By the early 1950s, it became its own nonprofit as churches throughout the US wanted to use their Bible-based curriculum. However, the strong evangelical roots kept the programming rigid and monocultural. As it then began to expand internationally, it began asking different questions about the needs of the cultures it wanted to serve. Now it has expanded to serving kids and training leaders in 135 countries throughout the world.[4]

Asking good questions is a skill that can be developed. Wherever you start, it's important to refine your question—to frame and reframe until you find the questions that dig deeper and gain further insights. J.R. Briggs, in his book *The Art of Asking Better Questions*, highlights a process pioneered by Toyota called the Five Whys.[5] This approach helped their engineers get to the root cause of a problem. The idea is to ask why and to not settle for the first answer you receive.

Why was our event poorly attended?

Because the invite was only sent to half the people on the list.

Why did the event invitation only go out to half the people on the list?

Because no one verified the list.

Why didn't anyone verify the list?

Because the team leader who normally verifies the list was on vacation.

Why wasn't someone else assigned to verify the list when the leader was away?

Because no one else has been trained on how to verify the list.

Why hasn't anyone else been trained on how to verify the correct mailing list?

Because the team leader has been too busy to train someone new.

This approach can be applied to many kinds of problems. Asking clarifying questions helps us get to the heart of the problem. Keep in mind the initial problem you are trying to solve as you frame questions. Asking the wrong questions can take us off course, wasting valuable time and resources.

Let's go back to the earlier example. We had seen tremendous fruit among older Russian-speaking Jewish people. Much of that success has been through in-home ministry—drop-in visits, door-to-door, care package deliveries. Older people were receptive to visitors and often spent more time at home. Young adults, on the other hand, were more difficult to reach at home and didn't respond the same way when dropped in on. So asking a question like "How can our staff get invited into younger Jewish homes?" would have limited possible solutions to in-home ministry only. That is where asking questions with your key audience in mind can help you clarify what you are actually trying to understand.

Finally, asking questions is important because it assumes we do not have all the answers. Through asking questions, we take a posture of curiosity and learning. If we want good design, we need to ask good questions.

ACTING ON THE RIGHT OPPORTUNITIES

As you explore insights into your key audience, it's important to evaluate which opportunities you should act on and which you should not act on. You cannot and should not act on every opportunity that presents itself. You need to determine which opportunities are the right ones for right now. Which opportunities could make the biggest difference to your community? Which could become a distraction from your core mission?

An excellent example of a company that acted on the right opportunities is Recreational Equipment, Inc. REI was founded as a co-op in 1938 by climbing enthusiasts Lloyd and Mary Anderson with the goal of making outdoor gear available and affordable. Their driving belief that "a life outdoors is a life well-lived" informs every aspect of their business model. Over the decades, REI has built a committed following of hikers, campers, bikers, climbers, and enthusiasts from every other outdoor group you can imagine.

In 2015, disgusted by the headlines of out-of-control Black Friday consumerism, REI launched its #optoutside campaign. Rather than take advantage of the mass shopping spree the Friday after Thanksgiving, REI closed all 143 stores, stopped processing online sales, and gave their employees a paid day to spend outdoors.

REI recognized which opportunities were in the interests of its twelve thousand employees and 5.5 million co-op members, and the company wasn't afraid to act on them. What followed was remarkable. The story blew up as news outlets covered it nationwide. Not only did REI go through with their decision, but 170 other retailers closed their doors that Friday and a thousand state parks waived their entrance fees as customers followed the company's call to #optoutside. They knew their key audience cared more about the beauty of being outdoors than whether REI opened on Black Friday. They seized on the growing public backlash against consumerism as an opportunity.

Recognizing good opportunities and acting on them is something good companies do, but good ministries need to do this as well. It is important not to short-change this process. The Design Stage is arguably the most time-consuming part of Mission Design. It takes time and attention to understand and unearth the needs of your key audience. If you have been ministering in the same community for years, it's important to not assume you have the answers. Strive to take a beginner's mindset: to remain curious and open as you learn about your audience and what they care about. Reading books and watching videos can be helpful, but there is no substitute for seeing for yourself.

Remember, Jesus took a face-to-face approach. He was born into a poor Jewish family, he spent time with people, he ate meals with them, he heard their concerns, he touched them, he even wept with them. He didn't do it to better understand them; he already knew their hearts. He was setting an example for us, and he drew close so his people could relate to him and could experience God's love in deeply human ways. Whether we've been in ministry for decades or are just starting out, his example points us to a posture of humility—the only posture from which we can live as ongoing learners.

IDEATION

Once you have identified one or more actionable opportunities that align with your core mission, it's now time to move on to possible ideas and solutions with your team. There are lots of ways to be creative, but brainstorming is an inexpensive, efficient way to generate new ideas. All you need are people, sticky notes, Sharpies, and a timer.

While brainstorming isn't an exact science, there is a common framework. Ideally the session takes place around a table, sticky notes and Sharpies are distributed, a timer is set, and a question is posed by a facilitator.

This facilitator doesn't have to be you, but it's important to find someone that can help keep things moving and will not dominate the session. Their job is to keep time, stay positive, contribute ideas, and keep the team focused on the problem at hand. They need to set a positive tone in order to create an environment where new ideas are shared. This is not the time to critique bad ideas, because sometimes even a bad idea can spark a great idea in a brainstorming session. It's the job of the facilitator to guide the process forward.

Ideally, brainstorming sessions should be short and focused. Use a timer to keep the team on track. A typical session can last anywhere from five to thirty minutes, though I prefer focused bursts lasting between ten and fifteen minutes. Choose a problem to explore. Framing a "How might we . . . ?" question can help your team focus on what they're trying to solve. For example, "How might we provide meaningful experiences for college-age young adults to explore ministry opportunities?"

During the allotted time, everyone writes as many ideas as possible, briefly taking turns sharing their ideas with the group. While you can brainstorm without sticky notes and Sharpies, they can be helpful in a brainstorming session because the small size of a sticky note forces members of the group to be concise. There's no room for a paragraph on a small square of paper! Sticky notes can be rearranged easily, which will be helpful later when it is time to organize ideas. Plus, the tactile experience of using a marker and paper unlocks a different part of the brain—with the added bonus of moving people away from their digital devices.

Beyond sticky notes and Sharpies, here are some things to keep in mind to make the most of your brainstorming sessions:

Rules lead to creativity. Though it may seem counterintuitive, limits and rules can nurture rather than kill creativity. Think about it: Which is more difficult? Giving someone a blank sheet of paper and telling them to write a story, or asking someone to write a short, funny story about a zoo for a group of toddlers?

Jack White of the White Stripes spoke of setting boundaries during the writing of their 2001 album *White Blood Cells*. They had five simple rules: (1) no blues, (2) no guitar solos, (3) no slide guitar, (4) no covers, and (5) no bass. It focused their creative process and enabled them to produce a powerful body of songs. Jack White described it as "the liberation of limiting yourself."[6] That is why we use a "How might we . . . ?" question. Something simple like that can focus the team and unlock the imagination.

Ideas can come from anywhere. It's a myth that the best ideas come from a select group of creatives. Good ideas can and do come from all over. If you are leading the brainstorming process, it's important to draw everyone out and to create an environment where new ideas are encouraged. Diversity of voices and perspectives will lead to unique ideas. If your team is a group of women, it is valuable to get a male perspective on the team. Ideo, the design consultancy, intentionally works with cross-vocational design teams that include professionals from a wide range of disciplines, including engineers, designers, scientists, and psychologists, to solve problems.

Another important reason to encourage everyone to contribute is for team members to feel invested in the solution. When everyone's had a chance to weigh in and be part of the creative process, that will ultimately foster greater buy-in from team members, even if the idea you end up using wasn't necessarily theirs. Anrea Belk Olson wrote in the *Harvard Business Review*, "Having employees buy in to change doesn't simply make implementation easier, but rather forges an immutable and reciprocal relationship which pays infinite dividends."[7]

Encourage wild ideas. As you've explored your key audience and gained insights into their needs, there may be dozens of ways to meet those needs. It's important to go as broad and extreme as possible while exploring potential solutions. The point of the brainstorming exercise isn't to just come up with obvious ideas that have already been explored. The idea is to think laterally: to allow your mind to wander in new directions and to allow yourself the freedom to have fun and consider outlandish ideas. In the end, you aren't going to use every idea, but you would be surprised how often unrealistic ideas can lead to good solutions.

Defer judgment. Avoid the temptation to correct or point out ideas that don't seem possible. The purpose of brainstorming is to encourage rather than stifle creativity. There is nothing that will kill creativity faster in a group than shooting down someone's idea publicly. That leads to an environment where group members feel judged. There will be time for evaluation later. I remember in one of our creative sessions, someone came up with the idea of handing out cold brew coffee and someone else pitched the hashtag #brewsforjesus. There wasn't a ton of enthusiasm for it, but we wrote it down. Later when bouncing around the concept with other people, it suddenly seemed more viable. Eventually we tested it out and were able to use it for years.

Stay focused. In the same way that deadlines often help people organize and prioritize their time, setting a timer during the brainstorming process can do the same thing. I typically set a timer from between five and ten minutes and explore ideas within that time frame. That doesn't mean you can't talk about more ideas afterward, but it designates that time for brainstorming and creates a degree of urgency and focus that your team will need to generate ideas.

In order to get the most out of your time, it's necessary to clarify what you are looking to solve. Try to generate as many ideas that relate to your "How might we . . . ?" question as possible. Make sure the team understands the question so everyone can stay locked in rather than drifting away from the main objective.

Goals can help focus the team. Feel free to set a goal, like shooting for twenty-five or forty ideas. You would be surprised by how setting a goal can help you push your team.

Don't get precious. Brainstorming sessions should emphasize quantity, not quality. Avoid getting hung up on an idea (especially your own), and encourage everyone to share their thoughts and then move on. It is important to keep things moving and not get too attached at this point to any particular direction. You want to avoid a dynamic where everyone is lobbying for their own idea. The objective is to work collaboratively and to unearth lots of possibilities at this point in the process. Don't be afraid to piggyback on someone else's idea. Feel free to use other ideas as a launchpad for your idea as it can lead to new solutions.

Practice. Team creativity and design are skills that can be developed. If you brainstorm together regularly, you will see gains. As the process becomes more familiar, your team will grow in their creative output. Over time you will learn to work together, to build on one another's ideas, and to collaborate better. Setting time aside for brainstorming sessions can help your team become more adept at problem-solving and discovering creative solutions.

SELECTING GOOD IDEAS

Once you have completed your brainstorming session, you should have a number of possible ideas to work with. In a good session you can come up with twenty-five or even fifty unique ideas. Collect the sticky notes and sort through them. You can often group ideas based on related themes.

For example, with the question we tackled in our New York ministry branch, "How might we provide meaningful experiences for college-age young adults to explore ministry opportunities?" we came up with ideas for programs including internships and short-term mission trips. But we also brainstormed producing materials like a devotional book for students. Another direction was to develop digital solutions like a website or a video series. Do your best to organize the ideas you've collected so that later you can quickly identify and prioritize which ideas you want to pursue.

I like to reorganize all the sticky notes thematically on a whiteboard or a wall where everyone can see. Choosing good ideas requires a clear understanding of what you hope to achieve. Once you have organized your ideas into similar groupings, filter them through the goals of your mission and the insights you have learned about your key audience. Which ideas really align with your mission and what you have learned from your key audience? You may be a homeless ministry that comes up with a great idea for an app to help students network on campus. Maybe it's a great idea, but probably not a great fit for your mission. Alternatively, you may have a great idea, like making students a free breakfast, that aligns with your core mission but isn't really needed by your key audience as they aren't up early enough for breakfast.

It's good to have the team weigh in on ideas at this point. Go around and ask the team to pick their top two or three ideas. Which ones seem to have gained the most energy and enthusiasm? Getting feedback from your team is helpful for a few reasons. First, they will have the opportunity to discuss and weigh in, which can lead to better decisions as you hear people's thoughts on why an idea might be more actionable. It can also lead to buy-in. Research shows that if people are able to weigh in, they will be more supportive, even if they disagree.[8] Ultimately, you need your team to get behind ideas if you are going to test out whether they can really work.

Remember, ideas are just ideas at this point. Some will be winners and some will be losers, and you won't know for sure until you have tested them out. Don't worry too much if you don't feel confident in your ideas yet. You can always brainstorm more or reframe the question you are trying to address. At this point you aren't married to anything. The goal is to find two or three actionable ideas to test out. We will look at prototyping in more detail in the next chapter.

SEEKING DIRECTION

Making wise decisions is crucial to the success of any endeavor. There are so many possibilities and potential ideas out there. How do we know which ones to act on? The Bible touches frequently on the subject of decision-making in the Wisdom literature. There are different ways to define biblical wisdom, but my working definition is being able to understand the nature of a situation and to apply

God's will to that situation. Put more simply, wisdom empowers us to make godly choices.

Scripture highlights that wisdom is to be prized above all. God himself is the source of wisdom, and he longs to impart it to us. He doesn't hide wisdom, nor is wisdom available only to a select group of people. Instead, wisdom is depicted as a woman calling out to us:

> Does not wisdom call?
>   Does not understanding raise her voice?
> On the heights beside the way,
>   at the crossroads she takes her stand;
> beside the gates in front of the town,
>   at the entrance of the portals she cries aloud. (Proverbs 8:1-3)

The imagery is clear. In ancient times, announcements were made from high places. Voices carry farther and people could hear from all over when called from above. Wisdom calls from on high in order to be heard far and wide. The picture of city gates is equally evocative. Cities are noisy, distracting places. Walking through the city gates, we are interrupted at every turn. But wisdom is calling in the noisy places. The crossroads, where the paths converge, is where we decide which way to go, what path we should take. Each road leads somewhere different. Wisdom calls out to us there too, guiding us toward where we need to go.

The good news for us is that wisdom is accessible. It longs to be heard, found, and applied. But it's one thing to discern between wisdom and folly, a good decision and a foolish one. What about when there are numerous good options? What about when you are deciding whether your church should plant a new congregation in another neighborhood, or if you should offer more services to the homeless community? All of these might be good decisions or bad ones, depending on the circumstances. There usually isn't just one right answer.

It is essential to remember that the proverbs in Scripture weren't prescriptive. They are meant to be understood through context and discernment. Proverbs 26:4-5 is a good example: "Answer not a fool according to his folly, lest you be like him yourself. Answer a fool according to his folly, lest he be wise in his own eyes." Which is correct? Depending on the circumstances, either option could be correct. Wisdom requires us to discern what a godly choice looks like in a specific situation.

Another important consideration is discerning God's will. Paul went on four missionary journeys. During these trips Paul traveled with his team to different cities. As a Jew from Tarsus and a Roman citizen, Paul was fluent in multiple languages and was culturally adaptable. God used Paul's experience and background to spread the gospel far and wide. When he arrived in a new city, Paul always began at the local synagogue. After all, Jews and God-fearing Gentiles would be found there. For obvious reasons, it made good sense to start with them. But how did he know which cities to go to and which cities to bypass? When to stay and when to leave?

Paul didn't entirely rely on reason. He sought God's direction in each decision. He spent time with his team seeking God's will (Acts 13:1-3). He believed spending time in prayer and seeking God's will were crucial to the success of his ministry. The implications are clear. If we remain open to God's direction, he is faithful to guide us. If he wants us to go somewhere or to someone specific, he will make that clear to us. Paul was guided through prayer to go in new directions and kept from going to places he longed to go (Acts 16:9, Philippians 1:13). Consider Ananias and Paul, Peter and Cornelius. If we are seeking his direction, he will guide us even when the path isn't immediately obvious to us.

Finally, we have God's Word to guide us. We know he has called us into his service "to do good works" (Ephesians 2:10). He has told us already to go and make disciples, so we don't need to wait until we hear a special word from him. He has called us to go, and he is faithful to direct our steps.

We will explore what those steps might look like for your organization as we take a closer look at the final stage of Mission Design, Land the Ship: Refine and Implement.

DISCUSSION QUESTIONS

- Now that you have insights on your audience, take time alone or with your team to brainstorm tangible ideas that might reach and serve your community.
- Which of the ideas that you brainstormed are good and can be easily prototyped, measured for success, learned from, and tried again? (Take a look at Appendix A, step three.)

TEN

LAND THE SHIP PART 1

REFINE AND IMPLEMENT

AFTER YOU'VE GUIDED YOUR TEAM through the Explore Stage (Understand Stage) and discovered potential opportunities during the Reentry Stage (Design Stage), it's time to bring the ship in for landing. This is where the rubber meets the road—where we move from ideas to action. In this chapter, we will look at how to prototype, measure, refine, and implement ideas into viable ministry.

The Jews for Jesus team knew from our exploration stage that we would need to address our image. It was clear that the majority of Jewish New Yorkers who knew of our ministry had a warped picture of who we were. But for those who hadn't heard of Jews for Jesus, we were basically a clean slate. The name even piqued curiosity. We recognized this for what it was: an opportunity.

As we began to consider the possibilities, we realized we might be able to address both groups at the same time. If we could find a way to reengage those with negative impressions of Jews for Jesus and build trust with those discovering us for the first time, we could slowly but surely make new inroads in the Jewish community. That meant making an uncomfortable shift: changing our public image. If we wanted people to stop perceiving us as religious extremists, we would need to pivot away from more confrontational styles of evangelism to more relational, value-adding approaches. We settled on presenting ourselves as relatable Jewish people with relatable Jewish stories, who also believe in Jesus. We didn't minimize that last part. We knew the gospel itself would be offensive. We just wanted to remove as many obstacles as possible so people could hear it.

The hope was that this shift would enable our team to engage with more Jewish students and help us find common ground so we could better relate to them. So instead of blitzing New York subway stations in identical bright-colored T-shirts and handing out thousands of tracts, we tried different approaches. We held regular creative sessions to brainstorm new ideas and tested them out weekly. We tried all kinds of things: collaborative art projects, sticky note message boards, opinion boards where people could share their views on various topics, pop-up Jewish holiday celebrations in Jewish areas, giveaways, and many other similar efforts.

Since the weather was getting warmer, one of our ideas was to give out free cold brew coffee to students on Jewish campuses. The initial rollout was bumpy. After all, we had zero experience serving coffee! But after a bit of trial and error, we figured it out. The reaction was promising. Instead of crossing the street to avoid us, people were lining up for cold brew coffee. It gave our team fresh opportunities to interact with people and to tell them about Jews for Jesus and why we were out there. Our team was starting to talk with Jewish people who had previously avoided us.

We set up Brews for Jesus stations on various New York college campuses at the beginning of the next semester. We went on to set up more stations at Columbia Circle, Union Square, Park Slope, Fulton Street, and Penn Station. Hundreds of people were stopping to interact with us each day. People were sharing pictures of our branded coffee cups on social platforms. We were creating different impressions of Jews for Jesus, and people were noticing. I remember an NYU student telling us their professor had brought one of our cups to his classroom as an example of good marketing.

#brewsforjesus was just one of our ideas. We had tried many different things. Some of it worked and some of it didn't. What's important is we weren't shooting from the hip. We were testing out ideas based on what we were learning from our key audience.

It's important to design with an audience in mind, otherwise most of us tend to gravitate toward things we prefer to do. Years ago, I received a call from a friend in another Jewish ministry. He asked if I would be willing to work on a series of apologetics videos with him. He desperately wanted to reach Orthodox Jews and thought this would be the best way to do it.

I wanted to help but I had some questions. "Do you know if they would watch apologetics videos? Do you know if they watch videos at all? If so, what do they like to watch?" The line went quiet for a moment. He admitted he really didn't know what they liked to watch or how they would find the videos, but he was excited to produce them. My advice was to explore first, to understand the community and to test out different approaches before sinking money and time into a passion project. It's important that we are aware of our own proclivities, as they will constantly pull at us. As we experiment and test out different ideas, we need to stay focused and keep what we have learned in mind as we design and prototype.

PROTOTYPE AND ITERATE

Start small. Once you have zeroed in on potential solutions, it's time to test them out. Eric Reis and Steve Blank, pioneers of the Lean Startup Method, popularized the idea of a *minimum viable product* (MVP). They urged entrepreneurs and business leaders to start small. An MVP may not even begin with an actual prototype. It might just be offering something on your website before producing it to see if anyone is interested, or spending five dollars to advertise an idea and seeing what kind of response you get.[1]

One of the most well-known examples of an MVP was Drew Houston's Dropbox video. Drew created a product demonstration video before he ever had a product. The concept of Dropbox was that users could share data across all their digital devices so they'd never lose a file. The idea was simple, but the technology would require months of development to get it right. Rather than start with perfecting his concept, Drew decided to see if there was interest. Before pouring months and months of time and energy into an untested idea, he produced a short, well-written teaser for tech-savvy early adopters to gauge the response. The video became wildly popular. Virtually overnight it amassed two million views and Drew received seventy thousand new sign-ups to the beta version.[2]

The point is that in the early phases of development, Drew didn't invest much. The purpose of an MVP or any prototype is to learn if an idea is viable before stakeholders commit significant time and money to it. Test at the smallest possible level and scale up only when you have measurable results.

Build a prototype. The idea of setting up cold brew coffee stations on campus was cheap and easy. We probably spent less than forty dollars on our first station. We invested in a cold drink dispenser, cold brew coffee, cups, a table, and a chalkboard with *Brews for Jesus: Free Cold Brew Coffee* written on it. The idea was to test out the idea so we could see how people would respond. Our working theory was that Jewish students would be willing to stop for cold brew and to interact with us. It was an inexpensive first draft that we could easily test and evaluate.

When companies prototype a new item, they try to get as tactile as possible. They look to build an actual prototype—a rough beta version of a device or product for people to hold, test, and experience. If a picture is worth a thousand words, a prototype is worth a thousand pictures. Prototyping is a quick and inexpensive way to explore the viability of an idea.

In ministry, a prototype is often not a physical object. It could be a program or an activity you need to test so you can simulate the actual experience people would encounter. I remember reading about an airline that was testing out a new kind of check-in line at the airport. They set up tape on the floor, had staff directing people, and tested a variety of ways for people to line up. This kind of prototype falls into another design discipline called service design.

Perhaps the best description for service design is an illustration. Service design YouTuber Mark Fonteijn says, "Imagine you have two coffee shops right next to each other selling the exact same coffee at the exact same price. Service design is what makes you walk into one and not the other, come back often, and tell your friends about it."[3] Service design is all about making what you offer useful, efficient, and desirable. The emphasis of service design is to create touchpoints or moments that help you establish a relationship with people over time. Prototyping in service design could be creating a pop-up space or testing out a new way for greeters to interact with new people visiting a church. It could be setting up cold brew coffee on a street corner or trying a new small group idea in someone's home. The idea is the same. Start with a small, quick, inexpensive version to test your idea, get early feedback, and determine whether that idea is worth pursuing. There are plenty of great ways to prototype. The more you test, the more you will learn.

Experiment. A few of us went out and set up our pop-up coffee station near Washington Square Park. The goal was to see if our idea had any potential. Would Jewish students stop and take coffee from random strangers on a street corner? Would they interact with Jews for Jesus? We weren't sure how they would respond. We had a working theory and we needed to test it out. It was a leap of faith. In some ways, every new idea is a leap of faith. Will people stop? Will they talk to us? Will Orthodox Jews watch apologetics videos online? Whatever idea you propose assumes some leap of faith. The idea is to close that gap as much as possible through prototyping and actual engagement with people you are serving. Understanding who they are and prototyping your idea will help you know whether your concept is plausible.

The first part of our experiment was to see if coffee would encourage Jewish students to stop. That part was easy to test. Lots of students stopped right away and took coffee. Apparently, coffee from a random stranger was fine as long as it was free. The next thing we wanted to evaluate was whether that free coffee would lead to interactions. Would they ask questions about Jews for Jesus, or would they just take a coffee and be on their way? Again, we were pleasantly surprised by how many people stopped and said, "I've always wondered about Jews for Jesus" or "I have never heard of Jews for Jesus. What is it?" We kept track of how many cups of coffee we handed out and how many conversations we had with Jewish people. The initial feedback we received was positive, so we continued.

When testing out an idea, it's important to evaluate what you need to learn. It's especially important to validate "leap of faith" assumptions. For instance, if the feedback you are receiving from parents leads you to believe that you can boost Vacation Bible School attendance through providing transportation, you should test your theory before renting the bus. One way to do this is to formally or informally poll parents on whether they would be interested in pickups and drop-offs. You could then charge a small deposit to sign up. Keep in mind that people will say all sorts of things, but they do not always follow through. That is why it is important to confirm interest before investing too much.

Here are some example questions that can be helpful as you determine whether your idea is worth taking to the next level:

- Did people interact or participate with your idea? Or did they ignore you? Being ignored doesn't necessarily mean the idea is a bad one. Your prototype may have not worked for another reason, such as poor execution or bad timing.
- Is your idea financially viable? Maybe it is a good idea, but the startup costs may be too expensive. You could give away free laptops and I'm sure people would stop and sign up for whatever you're offering, but you would run into money problems quickly. Also, it may not send the right message for your nonprofit to spend on something like this.

- Does it serve your key audience? Maybe another group is responding to your idea. Pay attention to who responds.
- Does it meet a need? Are people seeking this out? Getting feedback can be helpful here as you look to understand.
- Did they refer it to anyone? If someone comes the first time and then brings a friend the second time, that is a good sign. Anyone returning a second time is a good thing.
- Was anyone confused? Did they understand what you were doing? Some people will let you know they are confused, while others will just look bewildered. Pay attention to both.
- Do you sense God moving in this direction? Always bathe your ideas and prototypes in prayer and ask God for direction.

Maintain a posture of learning as you test out your ideas. Keep asking questions and stay curious as you continue to prototype. Trial and error is a great way to fine-tune your idea so you can move on to the next stage.

Unintended learning and unexpected opportunities. There is no better way to learn than to get out there and try it. Whether you succeed or fail, you will learn. Keep your eyes open; new opportunities may present themselves as you step out into the unknown.

In the 1980s, a missionary couple named Bob and Joyce Williamson relocated from the United States to Cochabamba, Bolivia, to do translation work with New Tribes Missions (now known as Ethnos360).[4] The work focused on ministry and translation among the local tribes. But while serving there, a group of Israeli travelers approached them with questions about the local indigenous population. The Williamsons invited them to tag along and showed them the area. They had a wonderful time together, and their guests returned to Israel.

Before long, groups of Israelis started to show up at their home. Little did the Williamsons know, these Israelis had told others about their work. Soon hundreds of Israeli backpackers were visiting them each year. They recognized these visitors for what they were: an opportunity from the Lord. Not only did they welcome them, but they expanded their ministry to Israeli travelers. They prepared Shabbat dinners and celebrated Jewish holidays with them. Eventually they recruited another couple to help in their efforts. By the time they retired, they had shared the gospel with over eleven thousand Israelis.

It's important to keep your eyes open to what God may be doing and to what you may learn. It may not be realistic for you to pivot like the Williamsons did, but it's important to be aware of opportunities that may present themselves along the way.

Trial and error. Launching a new prototype can feel awkward. When we started handing out coffee, we didn't know where to stand or how to serve people while interacting with them at the same time. But we stuck with it and started to learn. We changed where we stood, what we said, and what the table looked like. Over time, we noticed more people stopping, more people taking coffee, and, most importantly, more people interacting with the gospel.

Each time we went out, we made small adjustments. We ordered branded cups. We added lids and straws. We wore protective gloves. We used trays. We covered the table in a black tablecloth and printed professional-looking signage. We set up multiple touchpoints where staff would engage people in line. Each time we adjusted, more people stopped, and more people interacted. At one point we shifted to iced tea. We saw a drop in response. Coffee was more expensive than tea, but it was clear that if we wanted to stop more people, cold brew coffee was the way to go.

Soon we were running out of eighty gallons of cold brew coffee within an hour. People would line up and wait for us to set up each day. That was great, but the most important part was that we were learning how to interact with people as we served them. Initially, we were so busy that people just took coffee and walked away. But as we continued to prototype, we figured out how to slow the process down. We created an assembly line with people scooping ice into cups, others filling cups with cold brew, and others standing with trays. We had designated people at different points in the line interacting with those waiting for coffee. We got better at serving coffee efficiently, but we continued to keep in mind that this prototype was always in service of our overall vision. Our primary goal was to create positive impressions of Jews for Jesus to foster meaningful connection with Jewish students along the way.

Each version of our prototype was an opportunity to learn and to refine our concept. That is what makes iteration an effective way to scale an MVP into a full-fledged program. The Measure-Build-Learn feedback loop can help determine when a project is ready to move to the next level.

Regardless of the mission, we all want to know it's being accomplished. We want to know if our programs are working. We want to be able to tell our partners how God is at work in and through our ministry. In order to do so, we need to have clear goals and outcomes. Before we can hope to hit the target, we need to know what we are shooting at. In the next chapter we will look at the importance of measuring results and how to track intangible ministry outcomes.

DISCUSSION QUESTIONS

- Now it is time to prototype some of your best ideas. Take a look at Appendix C, a Prototyping Guide that asks questions both before and after your event or program.
- Did people interact with or participate in your idea? What elements?
- Does your idea resonate with your key audience? Does it meet their needs?

ELEVEN

LAND THE SHIP PART 2

EVALUATE AND MEASURE IMPACT

THE ONGOING EVALUATION of established ministry programs and testing of new prototypes are essential parts of Mission Design. Without defined goals or outcomes, leaders will lack a clear understanding of what is working and what isn't. Yet some ministry leaders get squeamish about quantifying ministry. It's easy to understand why. Reducing the work of the Holy Spirit to the number of decisions, baptisms, butts in pews, views on YouTube, or whatever else you count can feel deadening. Also, it may seem pointless to try to gauge spiritual impact since all fruit comes from God (1 Corinthians 3:6-7). However, I am convinced that measuring impact can lead to greater focus and increased ministry effectiveness. There is also biblical precedent for measuring ministry impact.

In Acts 2:41, Luke doesn't use *many* or *lots of* to describe the number of people who responded to Peter's message. He is specific: "Those who received his word were baptized, and there were added that day about *three thousand souls*" (emphasis added). Later in Acts 4:4 he tells us about the impact of Peter and John's ministry: "many of those who had heard the word believed, and the number of men came to about *five thousand*" (emphasis added).

The gospel writers are also uncomfortably honest when ministry wasn't effective. In Mark 6:5-6, we read the account of when Jesus himself was unable to perform miracles due to people's lack of faith. In Mark 9, the disciples were unable to heal a boy with an unclean spirit. Jesus cast out the spirit and healed the boy. They asked why they had been unsuccessful, and Jesus explained that in this case, only through prayer would they be able to cast the spirit out.

When we measure effectiveness, we become aware of the result of our efforts. Awareness and integrity in measuring results help us avoid the pitfall of success theater, which occurs when greatest hits reels are played over and over. This gives the impression of continued ministry vibrancy while masking a lack of current fruitfulness, like telling a story about someone that responded to our ministry many years ago to avoid the hard reality that our ministry isn't seeing fruitful results today.

When we track actual ministry impact, we get a thermometer read on where and how God is at work through our ministry. If the results are outstanding, it gives us reason to praise God and celebrate together. It also helps us know where to invest more staff time and ministry resources. When our ministries are unsuccessful, we become more aware. That awareness can create a holy discontent and push us toward intercession for our people and greater dependency on the Lord. Like the disciples, we must turn to Jesus and ask "Why?" when we aren't seeing ministry impact.

As with so many good things, it is possible to go overboard in tracking ministry results. God judged David after he carried out a census of the fighting men of Israel (2 Samuel 24). Numbers 1:1-3 and 26:1-4 emphasize that the census itself was not forbidden, but that Satan had been at work in David's heart behind the scenes. And David had succumbed to temptation by allowing pride to get the upper hand (1 Chronicles 21).

Like David, we can open the door to pride in *our* accomplishments. It's human nature. Whether it's the disciples arguing about who is greatest or the Pharisee looking down on the tax collector, pride is always lurking. As leaders, we must protect ourselves from allowing our identity to become rooted in our successes. Whether it's the size of our church, annual organization revenue, or the number of people who have come to faith through our ministry, there is danger in allowing metrics to define us. Without realizing it, we may begin to prioritize hitting the numbers over obedience to what God has called us to do.

The Bible cautions us to not think too highly of ourselves (Romans 12:3). When ministry is going well, it's easy to look around and compare ourselves to others. If we aren't allowing the gospel to work deep in our hearts, we may begin to look down on others and attribute ministry fruitfulness to our own leadership capabilities. Paul, one of the most effective missionaries ever, wrote, "far be it from me to boast except in the cross of our Lord Jesus Christ" (Galatians 6:14). While we long to hear Jesus say the words "Well done, good and faithful servant," we must remember that all ministry flows from who we are in Christ, not from our own abilities.

MEASURING WHAT MATTERS MOST

Years ago, while working in New York City, I struggled to get a read on the actual ministry we were having to Jewish people. There was plenty of activity. Teams were busy with different projects like summer camps, Jewish life cycle events, and evangelistic witnessing campaigns. All these ministry initiatives were designed to lead to one-on-one "visits." Visits had been the primary way Jews for Jesus had ministered to Jewish people for decades. Each visit was an opportunity for a Jews for Jesus missionary to sit down with a Jewish person for spiritual conversation, Bible study, and prayer. Through these visits, we have seen thousands of Jewish people transformed by the gospel.

I had been looking at our total branch visits for the month, which we had been tracking for years, but realized the numbers weren't telling me a clear story. I could see we were visiting with

Jewish people, but I couldn't tell whether we were visiting a hundred different people once a month or twenty different people five times a month. I had no idea if we were visiting the same people, or if we were meeting new people. It was also impossible to understand how deep we were going with them. Without additional information, I would never know.

Tracking ministry impact requires intentionality and thought. We must understand what we hope to achieve. We must clarify our ministry model and define what indicators will best help us determine whether we are on track. Writing up a theory of change can help you clarify what you are doing and focus your mission on those ministry activities that are most essential to accomplishing your mission.

THEORY OF CHANGE

A theory of change is a kind of blueprint that lays out the various activities of an organization and maps how they lead to mission impact. In creating a theory of change, we start at the end and work backward. In other words, we begin with a clear understanding of the purpose of the organization and the major outcomes it hopes to accomplish. Then we work back into the strategies that will best help us achieve those goals. We track midrange and long-term outcomes in order to know if the organization is trending in the right direction.

Figure 11.1 shows one way that ministry strategies can be tracked through short-term and long-term goals. Inputs are the resources used to accomplish the ministry. They include things like buildings, human resources, equipment, donors, and even your brand.

One good example of this is the work of the food pantry NYC Love Kitchen. Their mission is "to feed and mend lives through food, social services, and the bread of life."[1] They serve hungry people living in New York City.

They bring *long-term change* and transformation to hungry New Yorkers by providing the following:

- access to nutritional food on a daily basis
- access to services that can help people out of poverty
- spiritual encouragement

The *strategies* to accomplish their mission include:

- pop-up pantries that serve quick meals to people in impoverished neighborhoods
- food delivery to families throughout the Bronx
- services such as medical care, group therapy professionals, workshops, and classes to help lift people out of long-term poverty

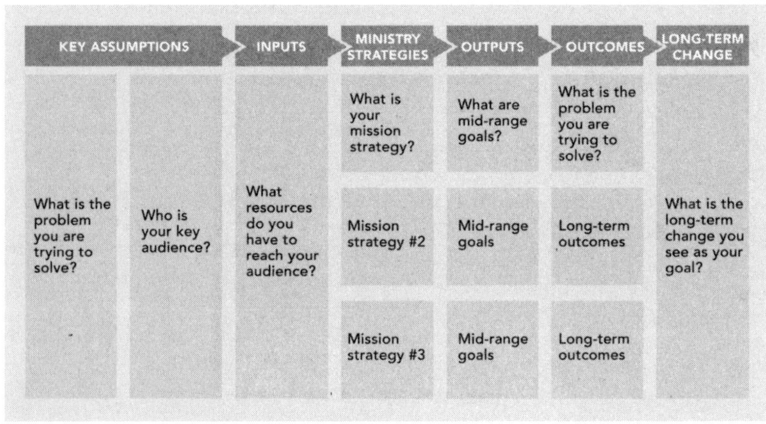

Figure 11.1. Tracking ministry strategies[2]

Long-term outcomes would include the number of people accessing services, the number of households being fed, and the number of partnerships that enable them to alleviate long-term poverty.

Short-term goals or *outputs* would be the smaller, shorter-term wins that indicate they are on track to accomplishing their long-term outcomes. These may include how many meals are served daily or households that have received groceries. These outputs help them gauge the number of people being fed. They may have additional outputs they use to tell them how often they feed people, like the number of meals served per week per person or number of people that have volunteered in a given quarter.

These kinds of metrics are called key performance indicators or KPIs. Using a theory of change framework can help your team determine which key performance indicators will help you track ministry impact and effectiveness. Tracking these indicators enables you to measure what's most important and can help you know if you are moving in the right direction.

INTANGIBLE OUTCOMES

Measuring tangible outputs like the number of meals provided is relatively simple. Intangible outcomes, on the other hand—like raising awareness around nutrition—are more complicated to measure and often require qualitative indicators. In his book *Good to Great and the Social Sectors*, Jim Collins tells the story of the Cleveland Philharmonic. Their big, overarching goal was to be recognized as a top-three orchestra in the world. The key to accomplishing this was through "artistic excellence." But how do you measure artistic excellence? They developed the following qualitative indicators:

- Are we getting more standing ovations?
- Are we expanding the range of what we can play with perfection—from clean classical pieces to complex modern pieces?
- Are we invited to the most prestigious festivals in Europe?
- Are tickets in greater demand, not just in Cleveland, but when we play in New York?
- Do people increasingly mimic the Cleveland style of programming?
- Do composers increasingly seek to have their work debuted at Cleveland?[3]

While these kinds of qualitative questions may not tell the whole story, taken together with quantitative data, a fuller picture begins to emerge. Jews for Jesus found it relatively easy to track, for example, the number of Jewish people to whom we minister in a given period. It was far more difficult to measure discipleship growth. We had to think through how to track discipleship indicators like godly character, generosity, and service to others. To do this we created a milestone system. During our visits, we noted when a person began to study the Bible on their own or when they started attending church, when they shared their faith with another person for the first time or when they volunteered their time to serve others. Together these gave us a sense of whether something intangible—like going deeper in your faith—was taking place.

It is important to keep in mind that a theory of change framework is primarily useful for ministry teams to map out how mission strategy leads to intended ministry goals and outcomes. It doesn't necessarily address things like communicating what is going on in the ministry with donors or board members. You'll want to translate your framework into a narrative you can use to communicate your change strategy and vision to your stakeholders. When people ask, "What do you guys do?" or "What is your mission trying to accomplish?" it is essential that you are able to tell a clear, compelling story regardless of who is asking. In chapter thirteen, we will take a closer look at the importance of storytelling and how to frame yours.

STAY ON COURSE

Tracking outputs and outcomes takes a lot of work. Perhaps the most challenging part is getting buy-in from your staff. The culture of Jews for Jesus has always been results-oriented, and yet we still struggled to adapt to tracking new key performance indicators. Our leadership was aligned around rolling out the new metrics and we provided training on how to track them. (See more on dashboards in the Scale and Implement section of this chapter.) We had many meetings and sent many reminders. Just when I thought the message had gotten through, I would discover staff had been forgetting to track ministry outputs. It took time because it was a change in culture, but our team started to get it.

It is incredibly important to be consistent when implementing the measurement of key performance indicators in an organization. Look for creative ways to reinforce performance measurement in each team. Ask program leaders to present performance reports in meetings. Take time to celebrate wins and highlight areas of growth. Set weekly, monthly, and quarterly goals to motivate staff.

Start small. You may only need to track two or three different indicators to start. Back when launching Massah in 2007, we sent fifteen people to India to minister to Israeli backpackers. We realized quickly that our typical approach for keeping track of ministry activity wasn't going to work. Back in those days, each missionary filled in weekly reports and measured the number of hours they worked, as well as visits, street outreaches, tracts, contacts, and decisions. Not only did ministry look different in India, but the fluid nature of backpacking through India didn't line up well with our standard metrics. As a result, we opted to track just three things: engagements (where we drop in conversation that we are Jews who believe in Jesus), conversations (short, gospel-related discussions), and visits (longer meetings where the gospel was fully unpacked). Not only was this manageable for the team, but it helped us prioritize what was most important.

Measuring outputs and outcomes can be helpful for a variety of things, including:

- Tracking ministry to specific key audiences
- Creating reports for different stakeholders, including boards and donors
- Allocation of ministry resources
- Knowing when to scale an MVP
- Celebrating wins
- Performance evaluation for programs or staff
- Rebuilding ministry programs
- Discontinuing mission programs

Though it takes effort, quantifying mission impact can be incredibly worthwhile. Without clear expectations around what success looks like or how to measure it, we will struggle to know if we are on track. How will we know if our youth leaders have been able to reach out and visit with more teenagers this quarter, or if our rehab center has seen an increase in people completing the program?

Like other organizations, ministries can become complacent. Ministers, like anyone, can slip into a comfortable groove. Things may be going just fine, but there is little sense of urgency to hustle or push the envelope. Without articulated vision and clear goals, we shouldn't be surprised to see ministries peter out. Look how many sleepy churches close their doors each year.

We know God is in control and knows all things. Tracking ministry impact will not help God remember what ministry is happening. It also won't help us "prove" the effectiveness of our ministry to God or make him love us any more than he already does. After all, fruit comes from him. Incredibly, he has called us to partner with him in his kingdom work, and we want to do whatever we can to keep ourselves and our teams striving for that prize. While metrics aren't necessary for God, they can motivate us and our teams to stay focused and on track. And they can help us give an honest picture to our supporters, partners, and boards of how God is at work through our ministry.

FEEDBACK

Jeff Bezos is famously quoted as saying, "Your brand is what other people say about you when you are not in the room." In order to establish trust in your organization and in the services you provide, it's essential to receive regular feedback from the people you serve.

In 1969, a network of several Jewish ministries sponsored a conference at Nyack College. The organizers of the conference felt it would be insightful to have a rabbi address the group, so they invited Sid Lawrence, a trained rabbi who served as a Jewish community worker in Kansas City. He was asked to speak about "The Image of the Missionary in the Jewish Community." Lawrence was brief and to the point: "The missionary to the Jews has no image in the Jewish community. We heard of you a long time ago. We never think of you."[4] Most people at the conference simply dismissed his comments. But Moishe Rosen took his words as a challenge. It became a catalyst that led to the eventual establishment of Jews for Jesus.

Unfortunately, leaders are often insulated from genuine feedback. Believe it or not, as difficult as it can be to receive, honest criticism can be even more difficult to share. If we shut down comments from those who share openly, they will think twice before sharing with us again. Proverbs 19:20 says "Listen to advice and accept instruction, that you may gain wisdom in the future." Try to make it easy for people to give you honest feedback. Ask people what they think and be prepared to listen without interruptions, unless you are clarifying their answers.

Whenever we prototype ideas, we need to seek lots of feedback. Feedback provides valuable insight as we look to design relevant and useful programs and services. Without feedback we will default to what we imagine people need rather than responding to what they actually want.

Getting feedback is an essential part of the learning process. Ideally, we need quantitative and qualitative feedback. Quantitative feedback could be, "How many times this past month have you received meals from us? How long did you have to wait to receive food?" Qualitative feedback would be, "How did our team treat you? What do you like about coming to our food pantry? What is the hardest part about coming here?"

It's important to get both kinds of feedback frequently whether you are testing new ministry programs or seeing how tried-and-true programs are working. There are lots of tools to help you get feedback. Surveys and interviews can be helpful, but informal feedback is valuable as well. Observe how people look when they wait to be served, or how they react when staff interact with them. What are their facial expressions? Do they look bewildered? Annoyed? Bored? While anecdotal, this kind of feedback also tells a story about your service.

Another tool that can be useful to capture feedback is the journey map described in chapter eight. Consider having staff fill these in as they track feedback they receive. Most digital services and platforms like YouTube, Google, and Facebook find ways to get regular feedback from their customers. They ask if people are willing to take a short survey or get users to give a thumbs-up or thumbs-down on a video. WhatsApp asks about quality after a call. Any point of interaction with your prototype can be measured. At the coffee shop Jews for Jesus runs in Los Angeles, we have an iPad set up at our register for people to provide feedback and sign up for local events. Feedback guides us as to how to refine our prototype, and it continues to shape the way in which we minister to people.

PIVOT OR PERSEVERE

Good leaders won't give up too quickly, but they're also able to let go when it's clear something isn't going to work. Eric Reis says in his book *The Lean Startup*, "When you hit upon something that is not working, you have two basic choices: change direction or keep going."[5] It's important to distinguish what Reis means by "change direction." He isn't referring to a pivot in vision but a pivot in strategy, like a change in the service you offer people or in the way you offer it.

There are lots of reasons why a prototype might not work. Maybe the time wasn't right or the prototype was poorly executed. In either case, the idea may be sound. Starbucks, a behemoth in the coffee industry, largely failed in Israel and Australia. They attempted multiple launches but never adapted to the local context. Both Israel and Australia had strong established coffee cultures, and Starbucks never bothered to adapt to what was already happening on the ground in those places. As a result, the company ended up having to close the majority of its locations and today largely serves tourists and visitors. While the Starbucks coffee model isn't a bad idea, you could make the case that both launches were poorly executed.

There will be instances when it's evident that your prototype may not achieve the desired results. If after testing different approaches you aren't seeing noticeable improvement, it may be time for a pivot. There are many examples of successful pivots in the corporate world. One vivid example came when Netflix pivoted away from DVD rentals and went all-in on streaming services while competitor Blockbuster went out of business clinging to DVD rentals in physical locations, a dying business model.

Another example is Odeo, which became Twitter and is known today as X. Odeo was initially a podcast service, but when they realized their revenue would be swallowed up by Apple, they pivoted to an instant messaging service. In each case, the picture was clear that they needed to change course. They would have gone the way of Blockbuster if leadership had not made the hard decision to pivot.

The ideal time to pivot is during the prototyping stage, but that isn't always possible. Sometimes a long-standing part of your ministry will become unsustainable or obsolete. Cultural, economic, and technological changes can affect your ministry effectiveness if you're not paying attention. That is why continual evaluation and some form of performance measurement is important.

And I cannot state enough how necessary prayer is to this process. Proverbs 3:5-6 reminds us that all of our techniques and strategies are secondary to our posture before God: "Trust in the Lord with all your heart, and do not lean on your own understanding. In all your ways acknowledge him, and he will make straight your paths."

SCALE AND IMPLEMENT

When you have proof of concept and a viable prototype that is producing consistent results, it may be time to scale into a full-fledged ministry program. Depending on the size of your ministry, it may require a full-scale rollout or some kind of beta version you release to continue testing. Keep in mind that going from a prototype to a first build is a big step. For a larger organization, you may have more time and resources available for this stage. You may be able to protype a new initiative and test the results while running multiple other programs simultaneously.

In the case of smaller organizations, the entire Mission Design process may require significant time and resources. A church struggling to run Sunday worship services may need more time and more volunteers to help get this process going. While there are no hard and fast rules about how much time and effort to allocate to this process, you need to build momentum. It will be unrealistic to launch a new ministry program, let alone measure the results, with only an hour or two of time invested.

When Jews for Jesus was testing new ministry initiatives, it was clear that our approach to tracking impact would be inadequate. Also, it wasn't mobile or team-oriented. We had a system we called the individual weekly report. The IWR tracked weekly missionary activity, but it wasn't designed for team leaders to see how their team was doing, set goals, or track impact. I began to consider alternatives. I explored performance dashboards online and mocked up my own.

I then built a prototype using Google forms. It was relatively easy to use, worked remotely on phones, and it was free. I had all our New York staff use it for our fall outreach that year.

It wasn't hard to get initial staff buy-in as they were eager to move on from the IWR. But when it came time to actually use it, many found it tedious or forgot how and simply gave up. They weren't accustomed to tracking gospel engagements and fluid ministry in real time on their phones. They had been used to sitting down once a week and completing their report on a computer. One major plus of this system was we could get data in real time. That could enable leaders to make decisions based on real-time information. But if staff weren't going to use it, it didn't matter how many amazing features it had. It would be a learning curve. I just didn't expect it to be so difficult.

Staff training was helpful but inadequate. I had to explain and reiterate why we were doing it over and over again. It wasn't something I had anticipated. To make things worse, I felt like I was constantly nagging people to use the system.

The following year I worked on a beta version using FileMaker and paid someone to build it for me. It was more robust and had an actual graphic interface. The staff used this system, which meant more ministry was being tracked in real time. But it was still cumbersome to log into and it had some annoying bugs.

I discussed the idea with our IT team, and they were enthusiastic about helping. We spent several months working on an initial design and product build to create our first legitimate performance measurement system we called Wingman. That process cost us more money, more time, and more staff energy than all the previous versions, but in the end we had our own bespoke performance measurement system. It took some time to get there, and it still isn't perfect, but we created a solution that works for us.

Whenever possible, take time to discover and scale your projects before spending lots of time and money on building a full-fledged program. Depending on the size of your project, you may not need many iterations. But with larger initiatives, testing thoroughly will help iron out the wrinkles before you design your first build. That way, when you finally decide to invest the time and money into a full-scale innovation, you will have a better understanding of what features you will need and which you will not.

DISCERNMENT

Building a sustainable, thriving ministry requires ongoing reliance on the Lord. Our Mission Design tools are limited in their ability to answer the most important ministry decisions, such as:

- Should we purchase a larger property for our church?
- Is this the right time to pivot in our ministry programs?
- Should our mission expand its footprint into a new country?

These are important questions that can permanently alter the course of our ministry. Decision-making in ministry requires looking at everything and discerning God's will and direction as you lead your ministry into the future.

It is possible to have an abundance of leadership/management experience and expertise but to have very little spiritual discernment. Ruth Haley Barton's book *Pursuing God's Will Together: A Discernment Practice for Leadership* urges leaders to not simply rely on management experts to run our ministries but to "cultivate a mutual commitment to discern and do the will of God together."[6] There are no shortcuts to this process.

She emphasizes the need for Christian leaders to practice "corporate discernment" through first investing in the spiritual formation of each member of the team. She contends that leaders must grow in their ability to discern the Lord's voice in their own lives before they can discern and lead others. She proposes cultivating spiritual disciplines around prayer, regular reading of Scripture, and silent listening to God. Leaders must learn to push back on the constant noise, activity, and performance-oriented drivenness that characterizes so much ministry today.

Taking spiritual retreats to get space and silence from the business of day-to-day life is a great way to seek the Lord. Full days and half days of prayer can be a regular way to put things before the Lord. I try to take time individually and in meetings to pray and study God's Word. Discernment is certainly a leadership trait, and yet it is also something I have seen work in a team setting.

Years ago, a number of us went to the campus of Brooklyn College to reach out to students. We were going to hand out tracts and preach the gospel, but something felt different. Instead of proceeding with our usual plan to fan out and distribute literature, we decided to change it up. We stopped and began praying together. Several of us began to pray and ask the Lord to help us understand how he was at work on this campus. Within five minutes, a woman stopped and asked what we were doing. We told her that we were Jews for Jesus and we were praying. She responded, "Can someone tell me more about Jews for Jesus?" I remember we looked around at one another, and one of us went to talk with her while the rest of us continued to pray. A minute later, someone else stopped and asked to know more. Within minutes we were all sharing the gospel with people. It was an amazing example of what can happen when we just stop and listen for God's voice in the midst of a busy day.

Mission Design without spiritual discernment can ultimately lead to unchecked, performance-driven ministry. That is a recipe for fatigue, burnout, and unhealthy competition as leaders feel the constant need to report bigger and better ministry results. While metrics and performance indicators can help us see where God is working, motivate us, and spur us on, they can also become an idol.

As leaders, we need to constantly check our hearts. Are we simply pursuing growth for growth's sake? Do we find ourselves comparing the budgets and number of staff in other ministries? Do we see partner ministries as the competition? If so, these are important indicators that we need to realign our heart with God's and seek to understand his desire for our ministry. To ignore it would be like sailing the ocean without using navigation equipment, compasses, or stars to guide us. Eventually we will run aground or simply drift without ever arriving at our destination.

Prioritizing God's direction and discernment doesn't mean ignoring all other wisdom or tools out there. Quite the contrary.

Integrating prayer into the design process can be meaningful and joyous as we seek God's wisdom and ask him to show us insights into our key audiences that maybe we haven't seen. We pray through and test out prototypes, looking for God's peace and blessing as we step out in faith. Mission Design is at its best when we put God at the center. He is the foundation of our ministry and gives meaning to everything we do. Prototyping, scaling, and implementing mission innovation isn't just about logistics or the technical steps of launching a new program. It is about the intentional and unintentional consequences of putting something new out into the world. It's about the cultural impact our innovations can have on the communities in which we serve and, as importantly, on the people in our own ministries. We shouldn't be surprised to find that some team members will struggle with innovation, no matter how good it is. Innovation is change, and change is hard. Finally, remember that innovation has the potential to change our ministries in powerful ways, and that what we launch today may make what we launched yesterday obsolete.

During the Mission Launch and Explore Stages, we looked at why our mission exists, where our mission is headed, and the people our mission exists for. We gained a deeper understanding of the needs of our key audience and grappled with different ways to meet their needs in the Reentry Stage. In the Landing Stage, we prototyped potential solutions and considered how to scale innovation and measure impact. In the final section of the book, we will look at how to put all the pieces together. We will consider how to sustain long-term impact in a spiritually healthy way and not get caught in the endless cycle of chasing the shiny new thing.

DISCUSSION QUESTIONS

- How successful was your prototype? Is it time to move forward with that idea or to try out a new idea?

- What are some of the short-term and long-term goals of your project? What actions do you need to take to meet these goals?
- What are the practical steps needed to increase the scale of your prototype to reach a larger audience?
- What metrics does your ministry use to measure impact? Are there other metrics that could help you gauge ministry effectiveness?

PART 3

PUTTING IT ALL TOGETHER

TWELVE

BUILD AND SUSTAIN A MISSION DESIGN CULTURE

I LEARNED TO DRIVE when I was twelve years old. My parents had both automatic and manual transmission cars, but my mother insisted I learn to drive on our manual. Her father had worked for Chrysler his whole life and made sure all his kids knew how to drive a stick shift. She said most people were bad drivers and she wanted to make sure that I had plenty of training by the time I was able to get my license. I was pretty small back then, so I had to sit on a cushion and pull the seat all the way up to the pedals. Our driveway was on a slope, so the car naturally pitched forward. She explained that when I let off the brake, I would need to ease up on the clutch while giving the car some gas. Timed correctly, the car would pull backward instead of rolling into our other car.

As you can imagine, I was terrified. The clutch and the gas were enough to think about. But I also had to remember to check my mirrors for pedestrians and other cars. I had to make sure I was in the correct gear. I had to remember to brake. I had to do all this while avoiding steering the car off the road. It was overwhelming to think about. I was pretty sure I could do one of those things well, but to do all of them at once seemed impossible.

The first thing I did when I was behind the wheel was let off the clutch too quickly, sending us both lunging forward. I stopped just short of our other car in the driveway. “No problem,” she said. “Start the car again.” Slowly but surely, I managed to reverse the car back out onto the road. I couldn't believe it. I was driving! It was a bumpy ride, but as time went on, my driving got better. Not only was I able to manage driving a stick shift, but I became more confident behind the wheel. The more I drove, the less I thought about each individual step. It all became second nature. I was no longer focused on my feet or the clutch. I was focused on where I wanted to go. I was finally able to enjoy the ride.

While Mission Design isn't simply a matter of timing or muscle memory, there is a learning curve. As you practice and repeat the process, you will see improvement. Not only will you become more adept at recognizing opportunities and brainstorming ideas, but you will learn how to weave them together as you innovate transformation in your organization and launch ministry initiatives.

After the successful design and launch of our Behold Your God Jerusalem campaign in 2018, we were excited to try a similar approach with other ministry teams and programs throughout Jews for Jesus. We found the process life-giving and wanted each team to feel the same excitement we were feeling. We were also looking forward to what innovations our teams would develop as they tried new ways to reach their communities with the gospel.

We asked each team to concentrate on one or two audiences. We gave them time to explore and understand their communities more deeply and encouraged them to pray regularly for them. We spent the next year walking with each team through the beginning of a redesign. Some jumped on board immediately while others struggled to adapt. At times the process felt bumpy. But over time, we began to realign many of our ministry programs with the actual needs of our key audiences. Not only did our teams develop amazing new programs, but they recaptured some of the spark and excitement of serving in ministry and began to develop fresh vision for the future.

Our rocket ship analogy reminds us that lots of necessary things need to happen for a mission to be successful. But all the steps that brought you to this point will lead naturally to the time when you'll put those pieces together and step into the future for which you've been praying and toward which you've been building.

SHIFTING THE CULTURE

The culture shift that took place within Jews for Jesus when we journeyed into Mission Design had a significant, even seismic impact on our ministry. We began to see problems as challenges that could be solved or as opportunities that could lead to better ministry. I was amazed to see how this mindset shift reenergized and reengaged our staff. We had always talked about why we did things the way we did them. But now staff were asking probing questions and exploring new possibilities. I cannot say at what point this shift began, but it was apparent that something powerful was happening underneath the surface. It felt like the beginning of something vibrant and exciting. The problem was, we had no idea how to sustain it.

One Saturday morning, Jesus walked into his synagogue. He opened the Isaiah scroll, read two verses, and gave one of the shortest messages ever: "Today this Scripture has been fulfilled in your hearing" (Luke 4:21). He had read from Isaiah 61, where the prophet spoke of a Savior that would heal the brokenhearted, proclaim good news to the poor, and set the captives free. This was Jesus' ministry in a nutshell. He believed in it so deeply he was ready to give his life for it. He talked about it. He taught about it. He sought out poor, oppressed, and brokenhearted people. He invited them to serve alongside him. He healed the blind; he touched the sick. He went to prostitutes, Samaritans, and tax collectors, each of whom was among the most reviled in Israel. He didn't live in a nice house, and he didn't wear nice clothes.

Jesus built a strong, lasting mission culture. It ran through every aspect of his ministry. While we don't typically speak of Jesus' work in these terms, his ministry had a strong cultural effect. After all, his church is still going strong, two thousand years later. Those he is attracting flock to him. Those he is not are repulsed by what he stands for.

Building a lasting ministry that can withstand change and volatility requires a strong, cohesive culture. Let's unpack what we mean by culture.

Organizational culture. When I first heard the adage, "Culture eats strategy for breakfast," I didn't understand what it meant. I had never given much thought to our ministry culture, nor did I see it as my responsibility to worry about it. This is because culture largely operates underneath the surface.

While culture runs through every part of an organization, we are rarely aware of it. But each organization and group has values, speech patterns, and unwritten rules about the way things are done. Every leader and every staff person plays a role in shaping the culture of an organization.

Perhaps the most widely used model to understand organizational culture was introduced by Edgar Schein, a social psychologist who taught at MIT Sloan School of Management. He described organizational culture as an iceberg with three levels: artifacts, espoused values, and underlying assumptions.

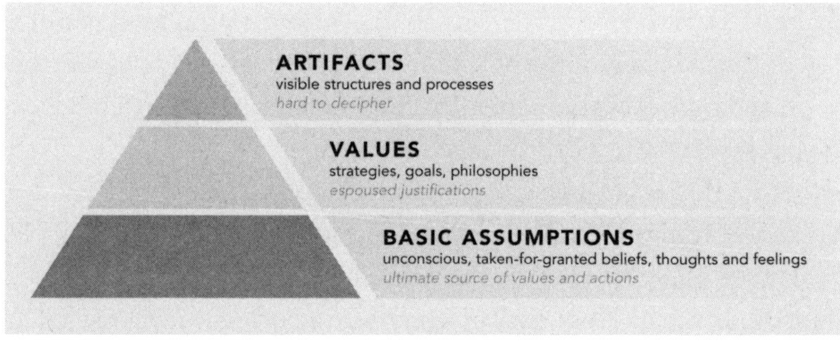

Figure 12.1. Levels of organizational culture[1]

Artifacts are the visible elements of an organization. These include the way an office is designed, logo placements, landing pages, dress codes, and how people answer the phone. Whatever you see when you walk into a church or ministry headquarters are examples of cultural artifacts.

Values determine the way people interact with one another inside the organization and how the organization is represented to the outside world. They include mission statements, vision statements, and core values. Values dictate the way staff talk about the work and how they behave toward one another.

Assumptions are the deeply held beliefs of an organization that often go unnoticed and unquestioned. They include beliefs about work, success, and failure. Assumptions are at play when you notice that one organization encourages remote work while another forbids it. Or why one organization emphasizes collaboration between employees while another organization seems to be fueled by interpersonal competition. Behind all these assumptions are beliefs about human nature and how the world operates. These deeper beliefs inform an organization's culture and form the values and artifacts of that organization.

Building a strong, lasting culture that values innovation is about more than new wallpaper or updated logos. It requires alignment across all three levels. When there isn't alignment, something will feel off. A church can brand itself as a warm, loving community, but if the congregational culture is built on the assumption that outsiders aren't to be trusted, it is likely that visitors won't receive a genuine welcome.

Unless we find alignment across our organizational culture's artifacts, values, and assumptions, our organization will struggle to find and sustain any clear identity. A misaligned organization will send mixed signals to those it hopes to attract.

Here is an example from my own context: a deeply held assumption in Jews for Jesus is that we work better together. Teamwork is in our bones. Since our earliest days, Jews for Jesus staff members depended on one another for strength as they faced opposition for being Jewish and believing in Jesus. We also know from experience that we can accomplish far more when we work together.

That is reflected in one of our core values: teamwork. This value can be found in our internal and external documents, in our hiring processes, and in our performance reviews. It reflects a value we care deeply about.

Our culture's artifacts highlight those values. For example, in our Tel Aviv branch office, you will see various-sized meeting rooms set up with conference tables, whiteboards, and staff in heated discussion as they collaborate on different projects throughout the day. These artifacts align wonderfully with our values and our assumptions about how missionaries should work together.

I cannot say our culture aligns everywhere, and I can't take credit where it does, but it is something our leadership team has intentionally worked on over the years.

Aligning organizational culture across all three levels is not a simple task. The most challenging part to address is assumptions. Schein argues that since we are largely unaware of what is going on at that level, it's best not to try to start there. As is the case with therapy or counseling, start with a problem. Addressing an issue that needs to be solved can help us get at the deeper, heart-level assumptions.

For years, I had struggled to understand the reactions I encountered when I helped launch new initiatives or ended long-standing programs. Whenever proposed changes touched on underlying beliefs or assumptions, team members pushed back in anger or frustration. Schein explains this phenomenon: "Human minds need cognitive stability, and any challenge of a basic assumption will release anxiety and defensiveness."[2]

That is partially why when I originally presented the Massah discipleship program, I faced some strong reactions. Without realizing it, I was introducing anxiety into the mix.

We should not be surprised to encounter pain points when addressing important ministry challenges. Leaders must approach these issues with sensitivity and patience. We need to give staff adequate time and space to process and wrestle through the deeper questions whenever possible. Remember, you may have been processing these changes for a while, so it's important to let the rest of the team catch up.

Here are a few ideas that can help:

Empowerment. Leaders play a pivotal role in shaping the culture of a ministry. This is true in big and small organizations. Smart leaders are able to rally a team to help in this important task.

To foster a culture of collaboration and empowerment, involve leaders and key staff in important discussions early on. This will help build their confidence, and they can then champion the vision to others. Inviting leaders to grapple with crucial ministry questions can pose challenges, but it is necessary to garner buy-in. It's normal to experience some pushback and disagreement within the team, so you want to provide healthy ways for staff to share their thoughts. Research shows that when people have a say in the big questions of an organization, they are more likely to embrace the outcome.[3]

Encourage honest discussion and feedback, as it will ultimately lead to stronger decisions. Patrick Lencioni, author of *The Five Dysfunctions of a Team*, urges leaders to promote healthy conflict and to get feedback often from teammates. "Ironically, most leaders of meetings go out of their way to eliminate or minimize drama and avoid the healthy conflict that results from it. Which only drains the interest of employees."[4]

By actively listening to your team, addressing their concerns, and working toward consensus, disagreements can be resolved within the group instead of aired in public. If a team member doesn't feel listened to, it is difficult for them to accept decisions and take ownership in a solution, idea, or vision. If they feel unheard, they might bring their disagreements to others in the organization or even to outsiders who often feed off the frustration and share a similar sense of contempt.

If you hope to get buy-in and deep engagement in the decision-making process, look for ways to involve your team.

Ownership. While leadership is ultimately responsible for creating and maintaining the culture of an organization, every staff member can play an important role in this task. Building an agile, innovative culture requires engagement across the organization. Ideas shouldn't only come from leaders.

Inviting your team to help solve problems can foster ownership and unleash creativity. This kind of collaboration can help ideas flow and solutions be discovered. Invite staff and volunteers to step up and even take the lead on initiatives when possible.

Innovative cultures cannot be overly controlled or stifled. Companies like Google, 3M, and Meta understand this and afford staff 15 to 20 percent of their time to work on side projects. Giving staff freedom to create can empower them and underscore that they are not a cog in a ministry machine. Another benefit is that side projects can feed new ideas that lead to fruitful ministry.

This requires balance, however, as staff can become siloed from the bigger vision and absorbed in their own ideas. Put parameters around how much time is allowed, and meet to discuss ideas together. Give direction and input. Set up brainstorming sessions where staff can work together on new projects. If a viable idea emerges that a staff member is excited to run with, let them. Look for ways to collaborate and integrate staff ideas whenever possible.

Listen. The culture of an organization is felt both inside and outside the organization, though not everyone experiences your ministry the same way. Leaders are frequently insulated from honest impressions of how stakeholders really feel. That is why it's important to get regular feedback.

Look for ways to survey staff, volunteers, donors, and board members to get a sense of how they see the organization. Workhuman provides some great sample questions for employee satisfaction, employee engagement, and workplace culture surveys.[5] Spend time visiting different teams to get a sense of how staff feel. Ask questions and listen. Don't feel the need to defend the ministry or respond to inaccuracies. Listen with empathy and seek to understand how others feel. We need timely, accurate feedback and input from staff and stakeholders if we are going to be able to adapt and change.

Use feedback. Soliciting feedback isn't enough to build a strong, innovative culture. Leaders need to pay attention to feedback they receive. People want to know you have taken their concerns and ideas into consideration. A 2021 Wakefield Research poll found that nearly half of respondents (45 percent) did not believe their feedback led to meaningful change.[6] In the same poll, 41 percent of respondents indicated they were looking for a new job. Failure to address employee feedback was highlighted as one reason behind the Great Resignation, the wave of people who decided to leave their jobs during and after the Covid pandemic. Look for ways to showcase staff contributions and show them how their ideas have been used whenever possible.

Communicate. Building and sustaining a Mission Design culture requires clear, repeated communication. Leaders need to cast vision and reinforce values over and over. Patrick Lencioni's 2012 book *The Advantage: Why Organizational Health Trumps Everything Else in Business* was a helpful resource for Jews for Jesus as we began to move toward a more innovative ministry culture. He argues that most organizations are already "smart," with good finance people, marketing teams, and other people in their workforce. What they lack is organizational health. They lack alignment internally due to politics and lack of clarity at the top. His model is simple:

1. Build a cohesive leadership team. They need to be honest, and care about the same things.
2. Create clarity. They need to understand mission, values, strategy, and desired ministry outcomes.
3. Overcommunicate clarity. Just when you think you have said it enough, say it again.
4. Reinforce clarity. Make sure you reinforce that message on every level of the organization.[7]

That is what shapes organizational culture. Tell people, over and over again, what you value most, and demonstrate that you really value it. Building a healthy organization from top to bottom requires not just talking about values but living them out. If you talk about values with your staff and say, "It's okay to take risks," then reprimand them when they fail, your people will not trust you.

Look for ways to reinforce those values in everything from public meetings, to one-on-ones, to performance reviews, to promotions. The more we can emphasize the amazing ministry breakthroughs we are seeing, the more people will be empowered and encouraged to follow us.

SIGNS OF ESTABLISHING A STRONG ORGANIZATIONAL CULTURE

There are no shortcuts to building a Mission Design culture. It requires time and patience, taking small steps in the right direction. It may take months or even years, but change will come, and you will know it when you see it.

Perhaps the most encouraging indicator is new talent. People are drawn to a healthy ministry culture with a vision for the future. When you begin to incorporate innovation into your DNA, people will be drawn to you. Don't be surprised if you discover people reaching out and showing up to serve alongside you. It may not happen right away. But eventually people will hear about what you are doing and look for ways to be part of it.

Conversely some staff may decide to move on. Expect some turnover if your ministry is in transition. While it is never fun to lose good staff, it can be a healthy process. Try not to take it personally when it happens. Help people leave well.

Finally, staff retention is a helpful indicator of a thriving ministry. While some departures should always be expected, constant turnover is never a good sign. Ministries that have a healthy, robust culture are often able to retain talent. They give employees a strong sense of belonging and satisfaction in the ministry that they do.

Changing culture is far more difficult than changing strategy, but they go hand in glove in Mission Design. I am convinced that the key to staying in step with global change and staving off decline is to incorporate innovation into the fabric of our ministry. Instead of playing constant catch-up, it's time to let innovation be the engine that drives us forward.

DISCUSSION QUESTIONS

- What are the artifacts, values, and assumptions of your organization's culture?
- What feedback are you getting from your team? Is the team taking ownership over the new vision or idea?
- How can you better support the leaders that you have under you?
- Are you seeing others who are interested in your vision and want buy-in? Why do you think that is?

THIRTEEN

THE IMPORTANCE OF TELLING YOUR STORY

IT WAS MY FIRST DAY attending the Taub Seminar, a graduate-level Jewish studies class at NYU. I was surrounded by a room of Jewish thought leaders. Secular, Orthodox, Reform, CEOs of Jewish organizations, and rabbis. I took my seat in the back, hoping to keep a low profile. To my horror the professor started the class by asking each of us to introduce ourselves, share briefly what we do, and tell the class how we hope to change the world. I wasn't expecting to have to talk about my faith or my work with Jews for Jesus in the first ten minutes of class. In the moments before it was my turn, I racked my brain for the right words. I knew each Jewish person in the room had their own version or understanding of Jews for Jesus, the majority of which I knew to be negative. Yet I was being presented with an opportunity to reframe it.

When it was my turn, I mumbled something about who I was and explained that I had grown up with Jewish-Gentile parents and had joined Jews for Jesus to help other Jewish people find out more about the rich teachings of Jesus.

I looked around the room as I shared and saw a few faces turn from uneasy to curious. No one scowled. No one told me to leave. It seems I had survived the first ten minutes of class. Fantastic! The real test would be how well I would relate to my fellow classmates for the rest of the semester.

I realized, however, that I hadn't been fully prepared. There was so much great stuff changing and happening in Jews for Jesus. I could have recited our mission statement or rattled off our different ministry activities. But I wanted to leave an impression that was personable, authentic, and memorable. Telling a story about my upbringing felt like the right thing to do in a room full of Jewish people. I only wish now that I'd had more time to prepare for it.

Framing and reframing the story of your ministry is an important part of Mission Design. Whether your ministry has been going strong for years or is going through massive change, the story you tell is crucial to how people see you.

We tell stories every day. We've been listening to and telling stories since we were children. We are so used to telling stories that we often don't realize we are doing it. Unfortunately, that also means we aren't always aware of how we sound to others or whether what we are saying resonates with those we are talking to. A powerful story can grab the attention of your listeners and help build trust in you and your ministry. It can build credibility and make mundane information memorable.

Research shows that our brains are actually wired for hearing stories. Story master Carl Alviani says, "We all have a strong, persistent sense of self, and stories essentially hitch a ride on the self, leveraging our self-awareness to lend emotional heft and durability to an abstract idea."[1] The areas of the brain that light up when we hear a story are the same areas that make us receptive and empathetic to other people. That is why people can spend ten hours binge-watching the latest season of their favorite show. Stories draw us in.

This is by design. God created us with hearts and minds that tune in to stories. Thousands of years ago, God commanded the people of Israel to retell the Passover story every year. No matter how many times we've heard it, that Jewish story of redemption is still able to captivate the hearts and imaginations of young and old alike.

Prophets frequently told stories. When Nathan confronted David, he could have just leveled with him. "David, the Lord is angry. You had Uriah murdered and you committed adultery with his wife, Bathsheba." Instead, in 2 Samuel 12:1-7, Nathan tells David a story about two men, a rich man with herds and flocks and a poor man with one small lamb. The poor man cared for his lamb night and day, and it became like a member of his household. The rich man, instead of killing one of his own flock to feed a visitor, took the poor man's only sheep, killed it, and offered it to his visitor. Hearing this story, David was outraged by the audacity and greed of this man. It was at that moment Nathan told him, "You are that man."

Storytelling is woven throughout the entire Bible. Jesus himself was a master storyteller. His parables were able to cut through even the hardest hearts and draw people in. The most important event in history was framed as a story. God didn't just give us bullet points of how he saved the world. He used four gospel writers to tell a rich, detailed story of how God loved us and of the son he sent to save us from death itself.

All ministries have a story to tell. But ministries going through deep change have a unique opportunity to reframe their story. Taking the time to reframe your story can be a powerful way to revive your brand. Whether leading a mission, a church, or a software company, we need clear, compelling stories if we hope to make a difference in the world. It is impossible to do the work alone. We depend on volunteers, supporters, trustees, and others who can champion our cause and spread the word. If we can't tell stories, we won't effectively engage the people we are here to serve.

Storytelling is a powerful tool that can help us build credibility and attachment to our mission. There are thousands of ministries out there. There are plenty of churches in your area for people to visit. Why should anyone visit yours? A compelling story highlights your values, your vision, and what makes you unique. When told well, a story can put a human face on your organization. A well-crafted narrative inspires and engages insiders and outsiders. For those outside your organization, stories can create a memorable impression. Internally, storytelling can help cast vision and create a shared sense of purpose and loyalty to your mission.

Several years ago, our leadership presented a report to our board of directors about our mission impact over the previous quarter. When it was my turn, I highlighted the number of gospel engagements, milestones, and decisions. I contrasted it with the previous year. I included nice visual charts highlighting growth. I remember looking out and seeing a room full of blank faces looking back at me.

Initially I was annoyed and started asking myself whether these people really cared about the work we were doing. But then I heard someone ask, "What do you mean exactly by engagements?" It dawned on me in that moment that I had not done an adequate job of telling our story. I had given them slides with stats and jargon. I decided that if asked to share again, I would need to do a better job.

Luckily, I got another opportunity. Several months later we were invited back. This time, when it was my turn, I told the stories of Jewish people whose lives were being changed through the power of the gospel. I shared how our ministry was being transformed as we were finding new ways to bring hope to Jewish people around the world. Instead of technical questions about my report, several board members commented on how encouraged they were and explained that they felt like they finally understood our new approaches to ministry. It was a valuable lesson on the power of telling a compelling story.

WHAT MAKES A STORY A STORY?

Certainly stories are important. But it is worth taking some time to think about what makes a story a story.

There are several common elements in stories. In its most simple form, a story sets a scene and puts us in the shoes of a character that has something they are trying to accomplish. They encounter a problem that they need to overcome. They either find a solution and overcome the obstacle, or they fail. It doesn't have to be anything as grandiose as Frodo needing to destroy the ruling ring in order to save Middle-earth from enslavement to Sauron. A story could be about someone who knows very little about cars but needs to buy one. They have a problem. Cars can have hidden problems and hidden fees, and salesmen are hard to trust. So they must find a solution if they hope to buy a good car. One business that uses this storyline to talk about what it has to offer is Cazoo, a dealer that takes the mystery out of selling cars. Every car is thoroughly checked, and all scratches and issues are disclosed on their website. There is no haggling; cars are all priced competitively, and all fees are disclosed up front. To make it even safer, Cazoo offers a seven-day money-back guarantee with the option to return the vehicle for any reason. Mission accomplished. Mystery solved. This person was able to purchase a car easily, safely, and economically.

Donald Miller, author of *Building a StoryBrand: Clarify Your Message So Customers Will Listen*, expands on this familiar structure.[2] He uses a storytelling narrative that begins with a character he calls the hero. This hero has a problem, and they meet a guide. That guide provides a plan and calls them to action that ends in success and helps them avoid failure.

Miller emphasizes that when telling your ministry story, that hero is not you or your ministry. The main character in your story should be your audience, the people you are trying to reach. In their world, this audience member is the center of their story, and they don't have time or interest in your story if it doesn't help them fulfill their goals or overcome their problems. Seth Godin, marketer and author of *All Marketers ~~are Liars~~ Tell Stories: The Underground Classic That Explains How Marketing Really Works—and Why Authenticity Is the Best Marketing of All*, describes the fact that it is always best to try to work within your audience's worldview.[3] Try to frame your story around their concerns and values.

In his book *Center Church*, pastor Tim Keller highlights the importance of starting with your audience's worldview.[4] In Western society, for example, the idea that God is gracious and forgiving is a more comprehensible starting point than something like, "God hates sin and is going to judge us all." Rather than starting with a foreign idea, try to find cultural common ground. If a particular group of people is already aligned with certain ideas and values, begin there and expand on that.

Paul's message to the people of Athens is a good example of this: "So Paul, standing in the midst of the Areopagus, said: 'Men of Athens, I perceive that in every way you are very religious. For as I passed along and observed the objects of your worship, I found also an altar with this inscription: "To the unknown god." What therefore you worship as unknown, this I proclaim to you'" (Acts 17:22-23).

Paul didn't begin with a Jewish understanding of faith and God. He didn't call out their idolatry or tell them how wrong they were. Instead, he told them a story about themselves. He shared about a devout religious people who worshiped an unknown God. And Paul put himself in the role of the one who could help them know that God. He positioned himself as the guide who could help them find out more about this unknown God.

The next part of a story is to frame the problem. Think again of *The Lord of the Rings*. Frodo, the hero of the story, has a problem. The ring he inherited is dangerous. If it falls into the wrong hands, the people of Middle-earth will be enslaved. Therefore, it needs to be destroyed. Every mission or organization exists to solve a problem or to meet a deeper need. We need to clarify what that need is—what we are offering to help them accomplish. While all problems have deep spiritual roots and all answers could be "Jesus," it is far better to start with a specific personal problem. Most non-Christians will find it irrelevant to start with Jesus as the answer to their problem when they are struggling to afford childcare or to feed their kids. How will this make sense if they don't know who Jesus is or how he can change their life?

It isn't enough to just appeal to reason. A powerful story should speak to both the head and the heart. One powerful way to engage the emotions is to share something personal. Maybe you also struggled with depression or addiction. Mentioning that I grew up in a Jewish-Gentile home was something other Jewish people could relate to since intermarriage is a common issue within the community.

Without an emotional connection to our story, we're going to lose our audience. What do they care about? What are they worried about? What will help them accomplish their hopes and dreams? It could be anything from finding a good car to something far more life-altering, like reconciling with their spouse. When we address a tangible problem, we can touch on the deeper spiritual needs people have. Jesus was a master at this. He healed a man born blind (John 9). The blind man's immediate need was sight, but Jesus was also able to address his deeper spiritual need. Jesus found him later and offered him the solution to something far deeper than his physical blindness.

In Miller's narrative structure, you and your ministry assume the role of the *guide*. Think Gandalf, Dumbledore, or even Cazoo. The guide is the one who helps your hearers navigate their difficult *problem*. Gandalf never took the ring from Frodo. Instead, he acted as a guide to help Frodo destroy the ring and save Middle-earth.

To be the guide, we need people to trust us. If we aren't viewed as credible or trustworthy, people will look elsewhere. Credibility can be established in different ways: endorsements from trusted ministry leaders, testimonials of how your ministry has impacted lives, and word of mouth can make a big impression, depending on your audience. Perhaps the most important way to build trust is through establishing a positive track record. Your ministry's story should include how you invest in and help those you serve.

The guide needs a *plan*. Without a plan, the guide is a bit useless. A plan is a solution to the problem or a way to help the hero on their journey. When telling your story, present your ministry as the guide that has a viable solution for the problem at hand and call them to action. This is where you explain how your ministry can provide hope and a way to ultimately help them overcome their problem and meet their needs.

Everybody wants resolution. A story without an *ending* is unsatisfying and will leave the audience confused. Resolution in the story leads to either success or failure. When we're crafting the story of our ministry, it's important to clarify the solution we are offering and how it can resolve the problem.

CLARITY

StoryBrand uses something called the "grunt test." Every website, email, message, or story should be clear and simple enough for even a caveman to grunt in agreement. Miller asks three simple questions when looking at anything from a landing page to an email campaign:

1. What is it that you offer?
2. How will it make my life better?
3. What do I need to do to obtain it?

If you have a clear answer to these questions, you have passed the grunt test.[5]

Clarity is crucial for your plan to appeal to others. If your audience gets confused by the details or by unclear steps, they will get lost. Chip and Dan Heath's 2010 bestseller *Switch: How to Change Things When Change Is Hard* talks about the importance of shaping the path because humans are lazy and tend to follow the path of least resistance.[6] Framing a clear, actionable story requires work. Blaise Pascal once said, "I have made this letter longer than usual, only because I have not had the time to make it shorter."[7] Taking the time to create an actionable, clear story for your organization is well worth the effort and will pay off in all sorts of ways.

Creating a clear call to action is a crucial step in your storytelling process. If people hear about a nice organization that can help guide them through a challenge, but they have no idea what to do next or how to get that help, we as storytellers have failed. It can be as simple as "Sign up" or "Connect with a coach" or "Leave contact info to have someone reach out." We need to be clear about what we offer and how to get it.

After the attacks in Israel on October 7, 2023, our teams, like most everyone else in Israel, were in shock. We didn't know how to minister or what people needed, but we wanted to help the thousands of people hurt, displaced, or lacking basic necessities. We began a coordinated effort to help those in need, especially the two hundred thousand Jewish and Arab Israelis displaced from their homes. We wanted to show the love of Jesus to people in practical ways.

It turned out our staff weren't the only ones who wanted to help. As they delivered care packages, visited hospitals, and cooked hot meals, they discovered others eager to find out how they could serve. They turned our event space into a distribution center for the community and registered under the Tel Aviv municipality. Our team was able to bring hope and sacrificial service to people at a very dark time. They were also able to create a landing page and a volunteer form to provide a clear way for others to sign up and serve. Before long, our team of fifty had grown to over two thousand Israeli volunteers serving the daily needs of displaced Israelis throughout the country.

In the aftermath of the attack, Israel found itself fighting a war on multiple fronts, including Hezbollah in Lebanon, the Houthis in Yemen, and a PR battle as people around the world were calling for the destruction of Israel. Many Israelis were frightened, had lost trust in their government leaders, and felt that the world had turned against them. In the first three months of the war, the number of orders for free New Testaments in Hebrew doubled. At the same time, our team in Israel served alongside volunteers who would never have given us the time of day before. Suddenly they wanted to know who we were and why we cared so much, which opened doors for us to share the story of how Jesus transformed our lives and gave us hope and a heart for others.

In the ministry story that we tell, we need to give people a simple, clear call to action.

PRACTICE

There is a kind of art to telling a compelling story in a clear, concise way. As with all art, practice can make a world of difference. Years ago, I started dabbling in photography. One day while out taking photos, I bumped into a professional photographer and started picking his brain for tips. His advice? "Take ten thousand pictures." The message was clear: almost no one is a natural out of the gate. We need practice to improve and grow, whether we're taking pictures or talking about the ministry we care so much about.

TED Talks are fantastic examples of clear, compelling storytelling. Speakers often address a problem and propose a solution within eighteen minutes. What people don't realize is that some of the best TED Talks ever given were rehearsed over two hundred times.

Musician Amanda Palmer's TED Talk, "The Art of Asking,"[8] was one of the most talked-about TED Talks of 2013. She explained that before delivering her talk she spent four months honing it. She wrote and rewrote it, delivering it to whoever would listen. She shared in hotel rooms, with friends, and with random strangers. She even shared her TED Talk with some guy at a bar.[9]

Test your story. Don't be afraid of receiving feedback or criticism; instead, use it to refine and strengthen your story. Not only will it help you craft a clearer, more compelling story, but it will help you know what resonates and what doesn't. Look to give tangible examples that can make your story real. The point is to be able to capture the amazing work your ministry does and to share that with others.

WRITE AN ELEVATOR PITCH

A helpful exercise to practice telling your story is to write an elevator pitch. The idea is that if you were asked on an elevator and you only had thirty seconds to share what you do, what would you say? The beauty of this exercise is it forces you to be concise, compelling, and clear. When constrained, we let go of unnecessary details and jargon and learn to make our point quickly. Take time to create your story, and practice sharing it whenever possible. You never know when you will be asked what you do and how you believe it can change the world.

Remember, you want to share how God is at work and the new life that is beginning to grow through the changes you have been making in your ministry. That story needs to be clear, compelling, and memorable. And it isn't just leaders who will be telling your organization's story. Staff, volunteers, board members, and many others will tell your ministry story. What do you hope they will say? What do you wish they'd avoid discussing—and why? While you may not be able to have everyone do the hard work of honing and rehearsing your ministry's story, it's important that they hear it, and hear it often. The goal is to make it their story too.

A well-known story about Christopher Wren, the famed architect of St. Paul's Cathedral, illustrates this idea:

One day, after work on his cathedral had begun, Wren walked among the workers unrecognized. He asked one of the workers, "What are you doing?"

"I am cutting a piece of stone," the workman replied.

Wren asked the same question of a second stonecutter.

"I am earning five shillings two pence a day," he replied.

He asked a third workman the same question, and the man answered, "I am helping Sir Christopher Wren build a magnificent cathedral to the glory of God."[10]

Anyone can tell a story. Stories have the power to capture our imagination and to change our hearts. Be encouraged; storytelling can be learned. Whether you are talking to trustees or to a classroom full of Jewish skeptics, there are lots of tools out there to help you craft and refine your ministry story for the world.

DISCUSSION QUESTIONS

- What makes your ministry or organization unique? What can you offer your "hero," beyond the gospel itself, that will help them grow?
- What do they need to do to obtain it?
- Take time to write a thirty-second elevator pitch (from 100 to 150 words) that might sell your key audience. (Think about their needs.)

FOURTEEN

COURSE CORRECTION

"HOUSTON . . . WE'VE HAD A PROBLEM."

These famous words were uttered by Jack Swigert, one of the astronauts on the 1970 Apollo 13 moon mission. Swigert and two other astronauts were two hundred thousand miles from earth when an oxygen tank exploded. The astronauts worked tirelessly under immense pressure to bring the craft successfully back to earth. They encountered problem after problem, but together with the team on the ground, they figured out a way for the astronauts to survive the ordeal. The story is a powerful example of staying calm in the face of unpredictable circumstances, and of how to pivot and make the tough calls when necessary. For this reason, the Apollo 13 story has frequently been used as a leadership case study in teamwork and improvising in a crisis.

As you and your team navigate the Mission Design process, there will be times where you will need to make some hard decisions. The disciples had no choice but to pivot after Jesus was crucified on a cross, raised from the dead, and ascended into heaven. Though he had told them these things would happen, they were not prepared for what came next. They had to pivot to where God was calling them. He had called and promised to empower them to be his witnesses, to make disciples, and to build his church.

In ministry, one thing is certain: change is constant. We will encounter situation after situation that will require us to address new realities and make hard decisions. Those hard decisions may fundamentally alter our strategy, and in some extreme situations may redefine the mission itself. The following scenarios are a few examples of where a course correction may present itself to your team.

STRATEGIC ABANDONMENT

There is an art to letting go while preserving the core. Years ago, while running the New York chapter of Jews for Jesus, I was speaking with my supervisor, Jhan Moskowitz. My team had been experimenting with all sorts of new ministry approaches, and I was proposing changing or even discontinuing certain long-standing programs. He urged me to be careful in what we were taking apart and what we were considering leaving behind. He said, "Remember, if you remove the carburetor, the engine won't work, right?"

"True," I said, "but what if we install fuel injection instead? Or what if we build an electric engine?"

He looked at me, smiled, and said, "I think you get my point."

When launching new mission projects, it's important to evaluate what you are trying to accomplish. Are you looking to improve on something that exists, or leave behind something that is no longer yielding results? There is always a balance. Keep in mind that there are only so many new ideas that can be added without sunsetting current programs. If you roll out new ministry without scaling back on something else, you will overwhelm your team. Management consultant Peter Drucker says, "The first key to innovation is the willingness to abandon the old so that you free yourself for the new."[1]

When letting go of old programs, keep in mind the pace of change for your staff. It's important to manage, since too much change too quickly can disorient and overwhelm your team. (That being said, if God is doing something new, be willing to pivot.) Try to find a reasonable pace when scaling back to help your team grapple with change. Remember, for many people, change will be perceived as loss, so their tendency will be to want to hang on to the past, draining energy from your mission and limiting new growth.

On the other hand, you may have an iconoclast or two on your team, who may be a little too zealous for dismantling old programs and systems. While that may free up space for new ministry ideas, it can also lead to cutting actual fruitful ministry, which is not the goal of Mission Design.

The strategic abandonment process requires significant prayer and discernment. Here are a few questions that can help as you consider whether it is time to let go:

- Does this ministry still align with our mission, vision, and values?
- Is this ministry still yielding fruit?
- Is this ministry meeting the needs of the community we are called to serve?
- Is this ministry draining resources that could be used for another promising area of ministry?

We don't want to let our own biases derail the Mission Design process. Certain staff will be afraid to let go of ministry that isn't really working because they feel nostalgic about the past. Other staff may be quick to hit the Delete button on the past to dive into something new. The key is prayer, discernment, and honest assessment. In my experience, legacy organizations will struggle far more than startups to leave behind languishing programs. They may even point to the fact that some people still benefit from them. A few customers aren't an indicator of a thriving business, nor are the few people still participating in a shrinking program a mark of ministry effectiveness. Remember that there are lots of good things your ministry *could* be doing, but you need to ask the tough question of whether this is what you *should* be doing.

MISSION DRIFT

Methods and programs may change, but it's important to not lose focus of the main thing. When we begin to reevaluate ministry programs and tinker with the mechanics of the mission engine, there is a tendency to question everything. But it isn't going to be helpful to completely dismantle the ministry's rocket before launching it.

Mission and values should be examined and nuanced from time to time in order to stay fresh and relevant. But be aware of how deep you go when you're cutting. Deconstructing your mission, identity, and purpose can create unnecessary angst and confusion for your team.

In Peter Greer and Chris Horst's book *Mission Drift: The Unspoken Crisis Facing Leaders, Charities and Churches*, the authors provide examples of organizations that stayed locked in and others that drifted from their original mission.[2] One memorable example was that of Harvard University. Founded in 1636, Harvard's mission was "To be plainly instructed and consider well that the main end of your life and studies is to know God and Jesus Christ." Today, Harvard's mission has nothing to do with knowing God or Jesus Christ. It is known for academic excellence. Greer and Horst propose safeguarding truth, not tradition. Methods, traditions, and preferences will shift depending on the context of the ministry. But your purpose, vision, and calling are truths you don't want to lose.

There are different ways to preserve the core truth of your ministry. Some organizations appoint staff with the express role of maintaining the mission focus of the organization. In addition, CEOs are responsible for carrying out the mission of the organization. This responsibility also typically extends to the board of directors. Some ministries even write up a charter to frame and protect the mission of their organization. In every case, it's important to keep the heart of your mission intact and beating strong.

ABORT MISSION

"For everything there is a season, and a time for every matter under heaven . . . a time to break down" (Ecclesiastes 3:1, 3). In some situations, God may be drawing a ministry to an end. A church or a mission may find themselves staring at the real possibility of closing their doors. This can happen for different reasons:

- Retiring leadership without a succession plan
- Financial instability
- The fulfillment of the mission
- The community you serve may have moved away or no longer require your services

In 2012, numerous organizations were launched to help the victims of Hurricane Sandy in New York City. Initially, there was a wave of support for these organizations as they rebuilt homes and sheltered displaced families. But as time went on, the needs of the community were met, and those organizations fulfilled their mission. So they packed up and moved on. This is common after natural disasters.

Dissolving an organization can be an emotional process, but it can also lead to something new. As vibrant and amazing as that first church in Jerusalem was, it didn't last. Other amazing ministries were birthed out of that first church in Jerusalem, but that original first-century church no longer exists.

It is unrealistic to expect any ministry to continue forever. God's kingdom is eternal; the ministries that serve it are not. When launching something new, few leaders consider their ministry's end, but if Jesus tarries, each and every ministry will need to consider whether it is time to close its doors.

If for one reason or another you are facing the possibility of ending a ministry, here are a few options to consider as you keep your core mission in sight:

Merge with another ministry. Your infrastructure may be limited, your team may be small, and you may not have been able to attract vibrant young leaders to take over for you, but you may be able to join another partner ministry and help them expand their work.

Donate your resources to another ministry. Your ministry may be effectively over, and you may be retiring, but if you have assets such as buildings or money, you may be able to do something significant for the kingdom. Consider supporting another ministry that aligns with your vision. Imagine the blessing it would be for them to receive that kind of material support. Pray about releasing and letting go. After all, these are the Lord's resources.

Dissolve and free yourself up for new ministry adventures. Perhaps you have been spending most of your time treading water, unable to do what you feel called to do. While God may be drawing your ministry to a close, he may also be opening up a new beginning for you. Letting go could be what you need to free up time and resources to do the work God has in store for you.

Whatever tough scenarios you may face, there is a way forward. The Apollo 13 mission is widely considered a "successful failure." The distress call from the Apollo 13 crew to Houston's Mission Control may have marked the end of their planned mission to the moon, but it was the beginning of a new mission to get safely back to earth. There will be times when things will not go as planned, where everything gets turned upside down. Whatever the circumstances you may face, remember that you can always pivot and adapt to the new situation around you.

Don't be afraid to improvise, pivot, and even abort your mission if necessary. Remember that God is the one who directs our steps. This is his mission, and he has called us to depend on him.

DISCUSSION QUESTIONS

- Are there places where you are drifting away from the mission? What steps can you take to bring back your focus?
- What things in your ministry or organization are yielding fruit? What elements aren't? What needs to be done for fruit to flourish?
- How has God surprised you as you've read this book and begun to think or prototype new initiatives? What next steps is he leading you to take?

CONCLUSION

THE MISSION AHEAD

IN THE EARLY DAYS OF SPACE TRAVEL, rockets were designed for one-time use. Each launch was costly and time-consuming. But over the past decade, significant advancements have been made. Rockets are now built to be reusable, carrying people and materials repeatedly into space. This is an appropriate analogy for Mission Design.

If we hope to establish and maintain thriving, relevant ministries, we must be prepared to launch and relaunch when necessary. In the book of Acts, we read about the emergence of a powerful new movement. The world, as the apostles knew it, had been turned upside down by the death, resurrection, and ascension of Jesus of Nazareth. The Spirit of God was now at work in the city of Jerusalem. Droves of Jewish people were responding to the gospel, but things were about to change in the young church again.

Peter, Philip, and numerous other disciples in Cyprus and Antioch encountered non-Jews eager to hear the gospel. Acts 10 tells us about a vision Peter received and his visit to a non-Jewish home in Caesarea. This pair of linked events forever changed his understanding of God's plan for the Gentiles. After witnessing the Holy Spirit fall on a Gentile family, Peter returned to tell his team in Jerusalem all that had happened. The church leaders convened and sought God's direction. Ultimately, they understood that a pivot was necessary. This pivot is detailed in Acts 15. The ministry of the church would now expand to include Gentile seekers. They had encountered an inflection point—an important change that led them to reevaluate their ministry model and seek God's direction again.

One modern example of a ministry inflection point can be found in the story of Operation Mobilization (OM). In 1957, George Verwer sold his possessions and set out with two college friends in an old Dodge van loaded with twenty thousand tracts and ten thousand copies of the Gospel of John in Spanish to share the love of Messiah with people in Mexico.[1] The response was overwhelming, so they returned the next summer and the summer after that. A gifted evangelist, George launched OM, which in time would spread to over 140 countries around the world. In the beginning, OM was founded as a proclamation ministry. Their teams would enter a city and concentrate on distributing tracts and other literature to as many people as possible. In discussion with Lawrence Tong, the current executive director of OM, he described it as more of a "hit-and-run" approach.[2]

As OM began to expand into Muslim countries in the 1980s, they faced significant challenges. The tracts and preaching methods they had previously used were ineffective in many Middle Eastern countries due to strict laws against missionary activity. It became clear that to share the gospel in these contexts, they needed to adopt a different approach. This led OM to experiment with relief and development work throughout the region.

At first, the reaction within OM was mixed. Some felt they were compromising the integrity of their preach-and-proclaim approach. After vigorous debate, it was decided that relief and development work would become a key part of the OM strategy. Today, under the leadership of Lawrence Tong, relief and development work composes 30 to 35 percent of OM's ministry.

In 2003, Verwer stepped down as executive director (though he continued to serve with OM until his passing in 2024), and the ministry continued to grow under new leadership. For the next decade, the mission grew from around 1,500 staff to nearly 6,500.

Tong noted that one of the primary reasons for that rapid growth was what he described as a "let a thousand flowers bloom" approach to ministry. During those years, OM opened the doors to a plethora of ministry approaches and strategies. But it came at a cost. When Tong stepped into his role in 2013, the mission had lost its way. A year prior, OM India had splintered away, and nearly three thousand staff had left OM. Tong and his leadership team knew something was amiss. They decided to zoom out and figure out what was wrong.

They conducted face-to-face interviews with 172 OM leaders worldwide, surveyed thousands of staff, met with many people who had come to faith through OM, and engaged a dozen key ministry partners. What they discovered was sobering. Leaders were struggling. There was a distinct lack of focus. Staff were restless and couldn't articulate a cohesive vision. There was a lack of unity throughout the mission.

One message was clear, though: despite all the issues, teams were seeing vibrant new church communities being planted among the least-reached people groups. It was evident that staff had a strong desire to invest in planting churches among the least reached. The problem was that church planting was not a focus of OM's evangelism strategy.

After gathering hundreds of hours of input from leaders and partners, examining what was working and what wasn't, and engaging in prayer, Tong and his executive team were ready to roll out a new vision. They believed this vision could bring focus and unity to OM's mission. They presented their findings, a new mission statement, new core values, and six key ministry initiatives to OM's broader leadership. Everything pointed to a new mission: building vibrant communities of Jesus-followers among the least reached.

After presenting this new vision to OM's leadership, the response was overwhelmingly positive. That vision, "vibrant communities of Jesus-followers," has come to permeate their work. It has been integrated into every aspect of the mission and has given their ministry new vitality and life. Sometime after the rollout, they sent out a survey to over four thousand staff worldwide. Staff shared that they felt more unified and had more clarity under their mission to build vibrant communities of Jesus-followers among the least reached.

This is an example of how the principles of Mission Design can revitalize a mission entrenched in history yet hungry to explore where God wants to take them. Tong and his team understood that while so much was going right with OM, God had more for them to do. The OM leadership team realized they needed to zero in on the sweet spot at the core of who they were, who their people were, and the vision God was giving them. They then took the time to zoom out, gather feedback, and explore what worked and what didn't. They spent time listening, praying, and seeking the Lord. When they had clarity, they rolled out their vision to the entire ministry.

In this book, we've examined the accelerated rate of change in the world and the challenges this poses to organizations as they strive to adapt and provide relevant ministry to their key audiences. We've explored the tendency for ministries to get stuck and how the Mission Design stages can help leaders and teams frame and seek answers to difficult questions. And we've looked at the critical choices leaders need to make in ministry, along with the reality that endings can lead to new beginnings.

We must be ready to pivot when necessary. Mission Design offers us a thoughtful, measured way to do just that. In addition, we must be attentive to the leading of the Holy Spirit while keeping a close eye on changes within our ministry context. Doing so will lead to new ideas and open up new possibilities. At some point, every organization will encounter change and experience decline. The key is to stay ahead of the curve and launch new organizational life cycles before irreversible decline sets in.

Continuous innovation and adaptation enable us to launch new cycles and create forward movement. Remember, it is far easier to launch a new organizational sigmoid curve while momentum is on the upswing. Once momentum is in decline, it demands far more energy to get something off the ground. Organizations tend to become more protective and fearful of losing what has been built in the past. When circumstances change, such as significant shifts in broader culture or the arrival of a new community in your area, it may be time to send your team back out to discover the best way forward.

Wherever you are on that organizational life cycle chart, God can do amazing things in and through your ministry. Mission Design can be a wonderful, life-giving process, as it has been for Jews for Jesus as well as other long-standing ministries and nonprofits that have undergone a period of reassessment and transformation. I am confident that no matter how big or small your ministry is, Mission Design can help you. Don't give up.

We all want to serve in thriving ministries. We want our work to connect deeply with the people we serve. That requires intentionality and understanding. Let us be like the leaders of Issachar, who "had understanding of the times, to know what Israel ought to do" (1 Chronicles 12:32). As you open yourself up to learn and dream, expect God to surprise you. God has equipped each of us to dream and create as we serve him. He is building his kingdom, and he has offered us the grand privilege of participating in that eternal work.

Let us keep in mind that this process of change and renewal is all part of our growth and development as leaders. He will use us to accomplish his will if we allow him: "And I am sure of this, that he who began a good work in you will bring it to completion at the day of Jesus Christ" (Philippians 1:6).

My hope as you've read these pages is that you have been challenged and inspired to step into the unknown and to explore what God wants to do in and through you and your team. My desire is that you would abound in fruitful ministry in whatever context you are in. My prayer for you is the same one Paul prayed for his friends at Corinth: "Therefore, my beloved brothers, be steadfast, immovable, always abounding in the work of the Lord, knowing that in the Lord your labor is not in vain" (1 Corinthians 15:58).

DISCUSSION QUESTIONS

- Which stages of the Mission Design process are you excited to begin? Which do you find daunting?
- Discuss together how you all feel about the Mission Design process. What did you find most exciting to jump into? What did you find most daunting?
- What has God revealed to you most plainly as you've read this book?

APPENDIX A

GOSPEL MESSAGING WORKBOOK

GOSPEL CONTEXTUALIZATION is all about sharing the message of Jesus in a way that intersects with an individual's unique context. The leadership team of Jews for Jesus developed a gospel messaging workbook to help our ministry teams discern how their key audience was intersecting and interacting with the good news. Here is a revised sample of the workbook that you may use as a tool in getting to know your audience and designing your mission.

STEP 1: IMMERSE YOURSELF IN YOUR AUDIENCE

Jesus entered into the everyday lives of the people he came to reach. The author of Hebrews writes that Jesus "had to be made like his brothers in every respect, so that he might become a merciful and faithful high priest in the service of God, to make propitiation for the sins of the people" (Hebrews 2:17). In light of Jesus' example, it is important for us as ministers to seek to identify and immerse ourselves in the key audiences we want to reach. This is a crucial part of understanding how to best communicate the gospel within each unique context. We want to free ourselves of any conscious or subconscious presuppositions we may have about our audience and avoid projecting what we think their day-to-day life is like or what their challenges are. By digging deeper, we may be able to gain powerful insights into the hearts of our key audiences and what is most important to them.

This step closely relates to the empathizing process of Design Thinking. Getting acquainted with the real experiences, needs, and feelings of your audience is critical in order to know how to minister to them.

Here are a few immersion approaches to choose from:

- Interviews (formal or informal)
- One-on-one or group discussions
- Focus groups (formal or informal)
- Surveys
- Watch YouTube videos, read articles, or follow blogs by people within your key audience
- Walk around a key-audience-populated neighborhood and make observations
- Go to events (virtual or in person)

A few tips for this process:

- You can always say to someone, "I'm doing some personal research on ________. Would you have an hour for me to pick your brain?"
- Try to really listen to people and not prompt or guide their responses to you. Keep in mind that people often reveal how they really feel in indirect ways.

Meaningful questions to ask your key audience:

- "If you could ask God one question, what would it be?"
- "What's the toughest thing for you when you consider faith and spiritual things?"
- "What do you think causes someone to believe in Jesus?"
- "Are things the way they ought to be?"
- "What's most important to you?"

- "If Jesus were walking the earth today, how do you think people would view him?"

Once you've completed this process, answer these questions with your small team:

- Which immersion ideas did you do? Describe your process.
- What insights did this immersion process help you gain?

Set a deadline for this first step before moving on to the next step.

STEP 2: TRANSLATING YOUR FINDINGS

After empathizing with and immersing yourself in your key audience, it's time to explore *how* you will articulate the gospel and connect it to your audience's real-life experiences and challenges. These prompts will help you script out phrases and paragraphs. Try to answer each prompt in full sentences; this will help you later in the process.

Your audience's needs:

- Who is your key audience?
- What are their surface-level felt needs? What are they lacking?
- What are the deeper, internal needs underlying those surface needs? Are there needs that your audience has that they aren't aware of?
- What are the surface-level idols that are worshiped (e.g., sex, money, comfort), and what deeper idols do those represent (control, love, acceptance)?
- What are some Scripture passages that speak to those needs?

Your audience's challenges:

- Make a list of the challenges your key audience faces (whether physical or conceptual, surface-level or underlying).
- Do any of these challenges seem to be rooted in spiritual idols or sin issues?

- What is the one challenge that you believe your team is best equipped to help meet in a practical sense?
- State a response to this challenge using a term like *ought* or *shouldn't* (e.g., "Ukrainian refugees *ought* to have the opportunity to make a comfortable home for themselves in a safe country" or "Ukrainian refugees *shouldn't* have to flee with no access to clothing, food, or shelter").
- How does the gospel speak to this challenge? What are some specific passages from Scripture you could use to address these challenges?

Connect and build trust with your audience.

- What are some ways you can demonstrate your approachability and trustworthiness in communication with your key audience?
- What are some ways you can communicate and confidently establish your competency in the areas your audience has felt needs?
- What are some statements you can make to demonstrate to your key audience your passion for your faith and for caring for them?
- What are some "testimony" statements you can make that help your audience see that you understand the challenges (surface or underlying) they are facing?
- How would you explain to your audience the practical ways in which your team will offer support to them in the face of their challenges?

Forward movement.

- What are the simple and practical steps that your audience needs to take to move in the direction of gospel transformation?
- How can you connect the shared values you identified earlier to the step you're asking your audience to take? What wording

would you use to build rapport and confidence in the support you can provide?

- What deep, internalized beliefs, fears, or concerns may prevent your audience from taking the next step toward Jesus?
- How can you alleviate these fears?
- Are there Scripture passages that speak to these fears?
- What indications do you look for that the Holy Spirit is stirring someone to take a next step?

Next, you'll need to motivate your audience to take action. People need to be encouraged and challenged to confront their issues, explore the deeper roots of those issues, and take action. Our collective job as ministers is to help stir their hearts to action.

There are a couple of ways to do this. At Jews for Jesus, we call them the front-door approach: a very direct action that is made in connection with an articulated interest (e.g., "I want to invite you to a talk at my church that I think you will enjoy because of your interest in social justice"), and the side-door approach: a more indirect action that invites someone to do something that opens up the possibility for further discussion (e.g., "I'd like to invite you to an art show I helped curate"). Consider and answer these questions with your team:

- What are some direct, front-door calls to action that you can make to your audience?
- What are some side-door calls to action that you can make to your audience?

Our goal is to help our key audiences realize *why* they need the gospel, understand its importance, and see what's at stake if they don't address spiritual problems in their lives. Honestly examine the natural consequences your audience will face if they do not overcome their challenges. What will happen on a spiritual level if their deeper needs aren't met, and their lives aren't transformed by the gospel? What are some Scripture passages that speak to these negative outcomes?

STEP 3: CREATING GOSPEL MESSAGING

Now that you've done the work of understanding the needs of your audience and asking the right questions to get you started, it's time to create gospel messaging. Gospel messaging is any way that we communicate God's redemptive plan using language that would be easily understood and relevant to our audience. The goal of creating compelling gospel messaging is to keep your key audience at the center of the narrative, ensure you are speaking to their challenges, connect their felt needs and the gospel, and point them forward to faith in Jesus. Here are a few ideas and activities your team can do to develop this messaging. This is by no means an exhaustive way to share the gospel—it is just to help you develop tools to utilize when you need them.

- Write a longer article that shares the gospel with your audience in a contextualized way.
- Write a script that leads a volunteer through how to engage in a gospel conversation with your key audience.
- Film a short video of a role-played gospel conversation between two staff, one of whom is playing a member of your key audience. You could also create a short video sharing the gospel in a contextualized way for your audience.
- Write a set of six to ten common messages or soundbites that could be employed on websites, social media, etc. to reach your key audience.
- Create three Instagram posts (select images and write captions) to share an element of the gospel that connects with your key audience's day-to-day challenges.

- Write an elevator pitch for what your team is doing: one for a member of your key audience, and one for people who support your work.
- Write a list of at least six phrases or questions that someone in your key audience might search for online if they were spiritually seeking.

APPENDIX B

IDENTIFYING YOUR KEY AUDIENCE

EVEN WITHIN YOUR KEY AUDIENCE, there will be nuances based on numerous factors such as location and culture. What are specific demographics (population, religious affiliation, age range, etc.) in your local community? Do your best to base your assertions on actual (not projected) data by looking at demographic studies, reading articles on current issues, attending events, or following related bloggers. This doesn't have to be a massive research project, but simply your team spending a few days diving into the wealth of resources available online.

The worksheets at the end of this appendix can be used to work through the following questions.

WHO ARE YOU ALREADY REACHING, AND HOW DID YOU MEET THEM?

Spend a few minutes thinking together about people that your team is currently reaching. Who are they—age range, professions, family structure, lifestyle? Take inventory of all the ways in which your team currently reaches people. Generate a list of all the evangelistic approaches you have successfully implemented.

WHO IS ON YOUR TEAM?

Next, look at your team itself. What are the areas of specialty represented here? Many members of our teams have a unique testimony, life experience, or skill set that gives them a natural intersection point with a certain audience. Do you have a family unit on your team especially gifted in reaching other fathers, mothers, and children? Someone from the background of the key audience you are trying to reach? A skillful artist? Someone who has conquered a major life struggle?

Compare these lists. Are there natural intersection points? Are there gaps on one list or the other? Perhaps there's a group of people interacting with you, but nobody on your team is poised to reach them. Maybe there are untapped skills on your team that could be used to reach a certain audience. Using this information, *prayerfully decide on your key audiences*.

What are the current experiences affecting your key audience? What are they struggling with or worried about? How do they seek fulfillment and joy? Draw from experiences and trends in your caseload, as well as general trends reflected in online surveys and studies.

List the broadest needs of each of your people groups on the left, whether they're felt or unfelt by the audience. On the right, list the specific ways in which your organization meets those needs. As you fill these out, you may notice gaps between the two. Is there a need you aren't fulfilling? Could you be expanding your ministry, utilizing more existing ministry resources, or partnering with another organization?

What sensitivities should you be aware of when speaking with your audience? Make note of those.

AUDIENCE and OUTREACH

I've noticed these demographics within my key audience

The people we're reaching	The ways we're meeting them

TEAM SKILLS and SPECIALTIES

The people on our team	Their skills and specialties

REACHING YOUR AUDIENCE

Their needs	How we meet them

APPENDIX C

PROTOTYPING GUIDE

PROTOTYPING IS AN INTENTIONAL PROCESS to help us refine our gospel communication. It helps us to:

- Use critical thinking in an ongoing way to uncover further insights about our audiences
- Explore areas for improvement and innovation in our ministry efforts
- Test out ideas so that we can commit the right resources to proven concepts
- Bring conceptual or theoretical ideas to life to help us understand their real-world impact
- Reveal our incorrect assumptions about our audiences and our biases toward our own ideas

The prototyping process has five basic steps:

- ***Empathize:*** Observe how people are reacting to your messaging and infer what their surface response reveals about what they may be feeling on a deeper level.
- ***Evaluate:*** Gather with your team, discuss your observations, and draw conclusions together.
- ***Ideate:*** Generate new ideas in light of your learnings.
- ***Redesign:*** Create new iterations of your messaging.
- ***Test:*** Return to engaging with your audience for more real-world feedback.

STEP 1: EMPATHIZE

Collect observations after events, outreaches, interactions, and conversations. The best practice is to write down observations immediately or within one day of an interaction. Your team should collect observations for as many real interactions as you can.

Not only is it important to *observe* how your audience is responding to your messaging, but you also will need to *infer* why they might be responding this way. For example, if we keep offering someone coffee and they refuse, we need to use that observation and infer that perhaps they don't like coffee, or maybe they are trying to limit their caffeine intake, and we could try offering them juice or water.

Use the empathy map as a tool to help you observe how people are reacting to your programs or your messaging and infer what their surface-level responses reveal about what they may be feeling on a deeper level.

Needs-based insights:

- Describe your key audience. Who are the people you are trying to reach?
- What are their felt needs?
- What insights do you have based on their needs?
- How can your ministry or organization meet those needs? What events or programs do you currently have or could develop to provide the answers that they need?

STEP 2: EVALUATE

After you have an empathy map filled out (or multiple maps), gather with your team to discuss your observations and draw conclusions together.

Evaluating one-on-one engagements:

- How did people react to our messaging?
- Did they understand the meaning of the words or actions?

EMPATHY MAP

Says	Thinks
← OBSERVE	INFER →
Does	Feels

FEEDBACK GRID

Liked/worked!	Change
Things that lead to gospel interactions Felt needs—idols—that were addressed	For example: The message was brushed off as irrelevant or not interesting; not enough intended people came, etc.
Questions	**Ideas**
Things that need clarification	For example: Next time we should make sure… Maybe try an event on…

- Did we have the opportunity to communicate the gospel?
- Did they have questions or objections we did not anticipate?
- How can we improve our communication of the gospel?
- What deeper matters of the heart have we been able to, or could we, address?
- What idols or deeper beliefs have we discovered?

Evaluating events:

- How many people attended the event?
- How many new people were present?
- How many people were from our key audience?
- Why did we have the attendance that we did?
- What could we do better to make this an event our key audience would want to attend?
- How do we think people felt at the event?
- Did our key audience engage with our team?
- How many interactions did our team have at each of the following levels: introductory, a conversation (including the gospel), a deep conversation (opened the Scripture together)?
- How can we create an environment where our key audience is asking the questions for themselves?

STEP 3: IDEATE

Now use the feedback grid to generate new ideas in light of your findings. You may also find that your observations reaffirm your gospel messaging, and you do not need to redesign anything but just keep creating new iterations of messaging as needed.

If you need to change some of your messaging, clarify the area you are looking to address by filling out the prompt "How might we . . . ?" and then allow that to lead to ideas using the prompt "How about we . . . ?"

STEP 4: REDESIGN

Create new iterations of your messaging. For example, this might look like:

- Writing a new Bible message for an event inspired by some of your observations and learnings about your audience
- Creating a new elevator pitch to be tested on a street outreach in your neighborhood
- Writing new social media content in light of what you have learned
- Changing the way your team describes a specific event or space

What will you test out with your next round of messaging?

STEP 5: TEST

Put your updated messaging out into the real world and report back to your team on the responses you observe. Record your findings and use these observations to return to step one of the prototyping processes.

APPENDIX D

DESIGN THINKING TERMINOLOGY

DESIGN THINKING

Design Thinking is centered on understanding people—their needs, wants, problems, and qualities—by understanding their culture and contexts. By understanding the people, we can understand what they need and create something to fill that need. This process usually occurs in the brainstorming stages of developing a business model and can be repeated to analyze the results and incorporate new ideas.

DESIGN SPRINT

A design sprint focuses on how a product is built. It uses the toolkit from Design Thinking to arrive at business solutions. It uses a small team of people who focus for a short amount of time. The process is to map out the focus problem, put pen to paper to come up with all the possible solutions, make a decision about which solutions to move forward with, develop the prototype, and then check the final prototype with the clientele.

LEAN

Lean startup is a methodology that begins by establishing a "canvas," which is the process of identifying the problem for the market and developing hypotheses to solve it. From there, the team creates minimum viable products (MVP) to measure success and pivot the product or service accordingly. It is highly focused on developing the market, a business model, and continually reevaluating the customer response and changing landscape until they have a product that works well.

AGILE

The goal of Agile is to speed up decision-making and development by focusing on context. Agile's philosophy is that iterative, incremental changes in product development lead, over time, to significant change. No matter what stage a team is at in their process, they bring value to their customers because they adapt and evolve quickly to changes in the market.

SCRUM AND KANBAN

Both Scrum and Kanban are tools under the methodology of Agile.

Often used by tech companies, Scrum doesn't seek to complete the design of a product but to keep on developing it. Someone oversees the project, another represents the clients, and the team carries out the development. Teams work in sprints to maintain focus.

Kanban uses some elements of Scrum, such as working in teams; however, it is a continuous process that is displayed in columns of "work pending," "work in progress," and "work done." It is meant to help companies optimize their workflow on projects and avoid bottlenecks.

COLLECTIVE IMPACT

Collective impact involves cross-collaborating on a big social issue with other nonprofit organizations. It describes an intentional way of working together and sharing information for the purpose of solving a complex problem. It helps organizations solve a problem together, which is more effective than one nonprofit trying to achieve social change on their own.[1]

NOTES

INTRODUCTION

[1]Kate Shellnutt, "Church Leaders Are Still Waiting for Volunteers to Come Back," *Christianity Today*, January 14, 2022, www.christianitytoday.com/news/2022/january/church-ministry-volunteer-gallup-survey-lifeway-wr.html.

[2]"Pastors Share Top Reasons They've Considered Quitting Ministry in the Past Year," Barna Group, April 27, 2022, www.barna.com/research/pastors-quitting-ministry/.

[3]Emily Brown, "The Great American Clergy Shortage Is Coming," *Relevant*, February 22, 2022, https://relevantmagazine.com/faith/church/the-great-american-clergy-shortage-is-coming/.

[4]Rachel Pfeiffer, "After 2,000 UK Church Buildings Close, New Church Plants Get Creative," *Christianity Today*, May 25, 2022, www.christianitytoday.com/news/2022/may/uk-england-church-close-anglican-buildings-restore-new.html.

[5]Ray Kurzweil, "The Law of Accelerating Returns," Kurzweil Library + collections, March 7, 2001, www.thekurzweillibrary.com/the-law-of-accelerating-returns.

[6]Kate Mayberry, "Third Culture Kids: Citizens of Everywhere and Nowhere," BBC News, November 18, 2016, www.bbc.com/worklife/article/20161117-third-culture-kids-citizens-of-everywhere-and-nowhere.

[7]Peter H. Diamandis and Steven Kotler, *The Future Is Faster than You Think: How Converging Technologies Are Transforming Business, Industries, and Our Lives* (New York: Simon & Schuster, 2020), 12.

[8]"America's Change of Mind on Same-Sex Marriage and LGBTQ Rights," Barna: Culture, July 3, 2013, www.barna.com/research/americas-change-of-mind-on-same-sex-marriage-and-lgbtq-rights/.

[9]"America's Change of Mind."

1. THE LIFE CYCLE OF AN ORGANIZATION

[1]Ruth Rosen, *Called to Controversy: The Unlikely Story of Moishe Rosen and the Founding of Jews for Jesus* (Nashville: Thomas Nelson, 2012), 194-204.

[2]"What Was the Jesus Movement?" Got Questions, January 4, 2022, www.gotquestions.org/Jesus-Movement.html.

[3]"Religion: Jews for Jesus," *Time*, June 12, 1972, https://time.com/archive/6839883/religion-jews-for-jesus/.

[4]"The Nonprofit Lifecycle: A Model for Making Smart Decisions," Georgia Center for Nonprofits, December 7, 2019, https://gcn.org/the-nonprofit-lifecycle-a-model-for-making-smart-decisions/.

[5]Mayka Katarina, "Decline Stage of the Product Life Cycle—How to Handle It," Eleken, October 2, 2024, www.eleken.co/blog-posts/decline-stage-of-product-life-cycle-overview-and-strategies, used by permission.

[6]Timothy Keller, "Why Plant New Churches?" The Diocese of Churches for the Sake of Others, October 17, 2019, https://c4so.org/why-plant-new-churches/.

[7]Katarina, "Decline Stage of the Product Life Cycle," used by permission.

[8]Susan Kenny Stevens, *Nonprofit Lifecycles: Stage-Based Wisdom for Nonprofit Capacity* (Wayzata, MN: Stagewise, 2001), 43-46.

[9]"Sigmoid Curves," The Money Engineer: Life Lessons, July 23, 2023, https://themoneyengineers.com/2023/07/23/sigmoid-curves-2/.

[10]Adapted from "Sigmoid Curves," The Money Engineer.

[11]Josh Hayden, *Remissioning Church: A Field Guide to Bringing a Congregation Back to Life* (Downers Grove, IL: InterVarsity Press, 2025).

[12]Timothy Keller, "Ministry Movements," *Timothy Keller* (blog), July 27, 2010, https://timothykeller.com/blog/2010/7/27/ministry-movements.

2. REACTIONS TO CHANGE

[1]John P. Kotter, "Accelerate!" *Harvard Business Review*, November 2012, https://hbr.org/2012/11/accelerate.

[2]John Kotter, *Leading Change* (Boston: Harvard Business School Press, 1996), 18-20, 139-42.

[3]Carolyn Dewar and Scott Keller, "The irrational side of change management," McKinsey & Company, April 1, 2009, www.mckinsey.com/business-functions/people-and-organizational-performance/our-insights/the-irrational-side-of-change-management.

3. GETTING UNSTUCK

[1]*Twenty Years of Congregational Change: The 2020 Faith Communities Today Overview*, Faith Communities Today, https://faithcommunitiestoday.org/wp-content/uploads/2021/10/Faith-Communities-Today-2020-Summary-Report.pdf.

[2]"Theological Vision," City to City UK, access date December 13, 2023, https://citytocityuk.com/theological-vision.

[3]Ronald A. Heifetz, *Leadership Without Easy Answers* (Cambridge, MA: Harvard University Press, 1994), 8-9, 73-76.

[4]Esther Han, "5 Examples of Design Thinking in Business," *Business Insights* (blog), Harvard Business School Online, February 2, 2022, https://online.hbs.edu/blog/post/design-thinking-examples.

4. LAUNCH STAGE PART 1: MISSION—WHAT IS OUR PURPOSE?

[1]Online Etymology Dictionary, *mission*, accessed December 18, 2024, www.etymonline.com/word/mission.

[2]Peter F. Drucker, "What Is Our Mission?", The Drucker Institute, 2018, https://drucker.institute/wp-content/uploads/2018/08/Reading_Drucker-on-Mission.pdf.

[3]James C. Collins and Jerry I. Porras, "Building Your Company's Vision," *Harvard Business Review*, September-October 1996, 68-69, www.cin.ufpe.br/~genesis/docpublicacoes/visao.pdf.

6. LAUNCH STAGE PART 3: IDENTITY—WHO ARE WE?

[1]Daniel Goleman, *Emotional Intelligence: Why It Can Matter More Than IQ* (New York: Bloomsbury, 2009).

[2]Ginka Toegel and Jean-Louis Barsoux, "Self-Awareness: A Key to Better Leadership: Self-Awareness is Crucial for Evolving and Finding Coping Strategies for Weaknesses. An Excerpt from 'How To Become a Better Leader,'" MIT Sloan Management Review, May 7, 2012, https://sloanreview.mit.edu/article/self-awareness-a-key-to-better-leadership/.

[3]"Women Poised to Effectively Lead in Matrix Work Environments, Hay Group Research Finds," Business Wire, March 27, 2012, www.businesswire.com/news/home/20120327005180/en&sa=D&source=docs&ust=1717328962700990&usg=AOvVaw1HBU_0_QckbnOXJwNYIpDE.

[4]Patrick Lencioni, *The Five Dysfunctions of a Team* (San Francisco: Jossey-Bass, 2002), xiii.

[5]Ruth Rosen, *Called to Controversy: The Unlikely Story of Moishe Rosen and the Founding of Jews for Jesus* (Nashville: Thomas Nelson, 2012), 189.

[6]Jim Collins, *Good to Great: Why Some Companies Make the Leap and Others Don't* (New York: Harper Business, 2001), 194.

7. LAUNCH STAGE PART 4: PEOPLE—WHO DO WE SERVE?

[1]"The Evolving Spiritual Identity of Jewish Millennials," Barna, October 10, 2017, www.barna.com/research/beliefs-behaviors-shaping-jewish-millennials/.

8. EXPLORE STAGE: EMPATHIZE AND UNDERSTAND

[1]Mark Tolts, "A Half Century of Jewish Emigration from the Former Soviet Union: Demographic Aspects," (Presented at the Davis Center for Russian and Eurasian Studies, Harvard University, November 20, 2019), https://daviscenter.fas.harvard.edu/events/half-century-jewish-emigration-former-soviet-union-demographic-aspects.

[2]Adapted from Rikke Friis Dam, *The 5 Stages in the Design Thinking Process,* Interaction Design Foundation (IxDF), 2024, www.interaction-design.org/literature/article/5-stages-in-the-design-thinking-process, used by permission.

[3]Albert Mehrabian, *Silent Messages: Implicit Communication of Emotions and Attitudes* (Belmont, CA: Wadsworth, 1980), 42-47.

[4]Amy Gallo, "What is Active Listening?" Harvard Business Review, January 2, 2024, https://hbr.org/2024/01/what-is-active-listening.

[5]Sarah Gibbons, "Empathy Mapping: The First Step in Design Thinking," Nielsen Norman Group, January 14, 2018, www.nngroup.com/articles/empathy-mapping/, used by permission.

[6]Sarah Gibbons, "Empathy Mapping," used by permission.

[7]Dave Gray, "Empathy Map," Gamestorming, July 14, 2017, https://gamestorming.com/empathy-mapping/, used by permission.

[8]Sarah Gibbons, "Journey Mapping 101," Nielsen Norman Group, December 9, 2018, www.nngroup.com/articles/journey-mapping-101/; "Journey Map," Service Design Tools (sdt), https://servicedesigntools.org/tools/journey-map.

9. REENTRY STAGE: DESIGN AND DEVELOP

[1]Victor Margolin, "Design in History," *Design Issues* 25, no. 2 (2009): 94-105.

[2]"Design Q & A: Charles and Ray Eames," Herman Miller, *WHY*, www.hermanmiller.com/stories/why-magazine/design-q-and-a-charles-and-ray-eames/.

[3]Design Kit, *The Field Guide to Human-Centered Design*, IDEO.org, 2015, www.designkit.org/resources/1.html, used by permission.

[4]"Portfolio: Awana," The A Group, www.agroup.com/portfolio/detail/awana/.

[5]J.R. Briggs, *The Art of Asking Better Questions* (Downers Grove, IL: InterVarsity Press, 2025), chapter two.

[6]Donald Sull and Kathleen M. Eisenhardt, *Simple Rules: How to Thrive in a Complex World* (London: John Murray, 2015), 78.

[7]Andrea Belk Olsen, "Getting Employee Buy-In for Organizational Change," Harvard Business Review, February 6, 2023, https://hbr.org/2023/02/getting-employee-buy-in-for-organizational-change.

[8]Olsen, "Getting Employee Buy-In."

10. LAND THE SHIP PART 1: REFINE AND IMPLEMENT

[1]Eric Ries, "The Minimum Viable Product: A Priner," Medium, April 6, 2015, https://medium.com/galleys/the-minimum-viable-product-a-primer-3d9a76dd5213; Steve Blank, "Why the Lean Start-Up Changes Everything," *Harvard Business Review*, May 2013, https://hbr.org/2013/05/why-the-lean-start-up-changes-everything.

[2]Rebecca Deczynski, "How Airbnb, Dropbox, and Reddit Got Their First Customers," Inc., May 31, 2022, www.inc.com/rebecca-deczynski/dropbox-airbnb-reddit-customers.html.

[3]Marc Fonteijn, "What Is Service Design: The Final Answer," Service Design Show, July 28, 2020, www.servicedesignshow.com/what-is-service-design/.

[4]Joshua Pex, "The 'Israeli' House in Cochamba," *Mishkan: A Forum on the Gospel and the Jewish People*, 38 (2003), 64-66, www.caspari.com/wp-content/uploads/2016/06/mishkan38.pdf.

11. LAND THE SHIP PART 2: EVALUATE AND MEASURE IMPACT

[1]"About Us," NYC Love Kitchen, access date December 19, 2023, www.nyclovekitchen.com/about-us.

[2]Adapted from Nesta, "Theory of Change," Development Impact & You (DIY), https://diy-toolkit.org/tools/theory-of-change/.

[3]Jim Collins, *Good to Great and the Social Sectors: Why Business Thinking is Not the Answer* (New York: Harper Business, 2005), 9.

[4]Ruth Rosen, *Called to Controversy: The Unlikely Story of Moishe Rosen and the Founding of Jews for Jesus* (Nashville: Thomas Nelson, 2012), 160.

[5]Eric Ries, *The Lean Startup: How Today's Entrepreneurs Use Continuous Innovation to Create Radically Successful Businesses* (New York: Crown Currency, 2011), 158-59.

[6]Ruth Haley Barton, *Pursuing God's Will Together: A Discernment Practice for Leadership Groups* (Downers Grove, IL: InterVarsity Press, 2012), 11.

12. BUILD AND SUSTAIN A MISSION DESIGN CULTURE

[1]Edgar H. Schein, *Organizational Culture and Leadership* (San Francisco: Jossey-Bass, 2010), 28. Figure adapted from Rupert J. Baumgartner, "Levels of Organizational Culture," ResearchGate, www.researchgate.net/figure/Levels-of-organizational-culture-examples-based-on-Schein-1997-p-17_fig3_227650803, used with permission.

[2]Schein, *Organizational Culture and Leadership*, 32.

[3]Carolyn Dewar and Scott Keller, "The Irrational Side of Change Management," McKinsey & Company, April 1, 2009, www.mckinsey.com/capabilities/people-and-organizational-performance/our-insights/the-irrational-side-of-change-management#/.

[4]Patrick Lencioni, *Death by Meeting: A Leadership Fable . . . about Solving the Most Painful Problem in Business* (San Francisco: Jossey-Bass, 2004), 229.

[5]Workhuman Editorial Team, "What Is an Employee Survey? Are They Important in 2024?," Workhuman.com, last modified September 5, 2024, www.workhuman.com/blog/employee-survey/.

[6]"New Poll of American Workforce: Millions Don't Feel Hard at Work," PR Newswire, September 28, 2021, www.prnewswire.com/news-releases/new-poll-of-american-workforce-millions-dont-feel-heard-at-work-301386677.html.

[7]Patrick M. Lencioni, *The Advantage: Why Organizational Heath Trumps Everything Else in Business* (San Francisco: Jossey-Bass, 2012).

13. THE IMPORTANCE OF TELLING YOUR STORY

[1]Carl Alviani, "The Science Behind Storytelling: Our brains are hardwired for narrative. Now we're starting to understand why," Medium, October 11, 2018, https://medium.com/the-protagonist/the-science-behind-storytelling-51169758b22c.

[2]Donald Miller, *Building a StoryBrand: Clarify Your Message So Customers Will Listen* (Nashville: Harper Collins Leadership, 2017), 76-78.

[3]Seth Godin, *All Marketers Are Liars: The Power of Telling Authentic Stories in a Low-Trust World* (New York: Penguin, 2009), 69-71.

[4]Timothy Keller, *Center Church: Doing Balanced, Gospel-Centered Ministry in Your City* (Grand Rapids, MI: Zondervan, 2012).

[5]James Hannan, "What Is the Grunt Text? A Lesson in StoryBrand Clarity," Results & Co, February 22, 2021, https://resultsandco.com.au/blog/storybrand-grunt-test-donald-miller.

[6]Chip Heath and Dan Heath, *Switch: How to Change Things When Change Is Hard* (New York: Broadway Books, 2010).

[7]Blaise Pascal, *The Provincial Letters*, Letter 16, 1657.

[8]Amanda Palmer, "The Art of Asking," TED Talks, February 2013, video, www.ted.com/talks/amanda_palmer_the_art_of_asking.

[9]Carmine Gallo, "The One Habit That Brilliant TED Speakers Practice Up To 200 Times," *Forbes*, March 17, 2014, www.forbes.com/sites/carminegallo/2014/03/17/the-one-habit-that-brilliant-ted-speakers-practice-up-to-200-times/.

[10]Bruce Barton, *What a Man Can Believe* (Indianapolis: Bobs-Merrill, 1927), 252-53.

14. COURSE CORRECTION

[1]Joseph A. Maciariello, *A Year with Peter Drucker: 52 Weeks of Coaching for Leadership Effectiveness* (New York: HarperCollins, 2014), 170-76.

[2]Peter Greer and Chris Horst, *Mission Drift: The Unspoken Crisis Facing Leaders, Charities, and Churches* (Minneapolis: Bethany House, 2014), 16-17.

CONCLUSION: THE MISSION AHEAD

[1]Justin Taylor, "George Verwer (1938–2023)," *Between Two Worlds* (blog), The Gospel Coalition, April 15, 2023, www.thegospelcoalition.org/blogs/justin-taylor/george-verwer-1938-2023/.

[2]Lawrence Tong, conversation with the author, December 20, 2024.

APPENDIX D: DESIGN THINKING TERMINOLOGY

[1]"Collective Impact Collaborations," The Bridgespan Group, January 15, 2016, www.bridgespan.org/insights/collective-impact-collaborations.